G000075773

THE A-Z OF COUNTRY AND IRISH STARS

BRIAN CARTHY

GILL AND MACMILLAN
AND
RADIO TELEFÍS ÉIREANN

Published in Ireland by
Gill and Macmillan Ltd
Goldenbridge
Dublin 8
and
Radio Telefís Éireann
Donnybrook
Dublin 4
© Brian Carthy 1991
Print origination by
Seton Music Graphics Ltd, Bantry, Co. Cork
Printed by Colour Books Ltd, Dublin

British Library Cataloguing in Publication Data
Carthy, Brian
The A–Z of country and Irish stars.
I. Title
781.64209415
ISBN 0–7171–1882–7

Front cover illustrations show (clockwise from the top left):
Daniel O'Donnell; Foster & Allen; Big Tom;
Susan McCann; Mary Duff; and Louise Morrissey.

CONTENTS

INTRODUCTION

There are many reasons why I decided to write this book, not least the enormous response to my regular Country 'N' Irish column in the *RTE Guide*. But it goes much much deeper than that. My love of Country and Irish music stretches back to my earliest years growing up in the townland of Ballymore about three miles from Strokestown, in County Roscommon. Life was different then, over twenty years ago. It was an era the showbands ruled and the whole world seemed young. Brendan Bowyer was hitting the high notes with *The Hucklebuck*, Butch Moore was *Walking The Streets In The Rain*, Dickie Rock was telling us about *The Candy Store On The Corner*, Larry Cunningham was visiting *Lovely Leitrim*, while Joe Dolan was, and indeed remained, the *Westmeath Bachelor*. Some things never change. The legendary Michael O'Hehir was the voice of sport and a young girl from Kincasslagh, County Donegal made it into the Irish charts with *Bonnie Irish Boy*. Her name was Margo.

Back then summer holidays were spent around the foothills of Sliabh Bán with family and friends playing football and hurling, making the hay and saving the turf. Then there was Ballybeg Carnival, one of the social highlights of the year. Although too young to attend the dances, I would stay up late listening to the music, sitting on a stone outside our house, situated some distance away. I remember the excitement when Pat McGeegan, now sadly deceased, appeared at the carnival. A short time before that Pat had represented Ireland in the Eurovision Song Contest singing *Chance Of A Lifetime*, and there was a great sense of pride at the thought of a superstar entertaining us in Ballybeg carnival. That memory is still fresh in my mind.

The music of Margo, Brian Coll, Larry Cunningham, Big Tom, Ray Lynam, Tommy Drennan, Philomena Begley, Johnny McEvoy and Brendan Shine instilled in me a love of all things Country and Irish, and now, many years later, I am honoured to be counted among their friends. They were just some of the household names talented enough to survive the bad times when ballrooms closed and disco mania took over.

I first started writing about matters Country and Irish for provincial papers nearly fifteen years ago and I am delighted to report that the music is still as popular as ever despite the changing trends. In fact, there has been a tremendous upsurge of interest in Country music of late and this has manifested itself in many ways, most notably in the emergence of many new singers like Declan Nerney, Mick Flavin, Kathy Durkan, Anne Breen, Louise Morrissey, John Hogan, Michael O'Brien, Mary Duff, Paddy O'Brien and, of course, Daniel O'Donnell, the biggest name in Country music, not just in Ireland but also in Britain.

This book, which profiles over seventy artists of differing musical persuasions, I dedicate to music lovers everywhere: those who remember the Sixties and Seventies and those who are just beginning to appreciate music in whatever form it takes.

For me, music, like sport, has a mystique all its own. Long may we live to enjoy it.

Brian Carthy

THE A-Z OF COUNTRY AND IRISH STARS

Á I N E

> *As long as you have your family behind you, you can overcome all obstacles*

Despite the fact that Áine has been a professional singer for only a comparatively short time, she seems destined for stardom. Already she has emerged from relative obscurity to establish herself as an entertainer of some considerable stature.

From a very early age Áine Cromie, a native of Killean, County Armagh, displayed great potential and could be seen regularly, guitar in hand, competing at many local competitions.

From the time she won her very first talent competition at the age of nine, Áine's heart was set on a musical career. The all-important musical breakthrough, which so many strive for but never quite attain, came in 1989 when she was approached by promoter Tony Loughman while performing her own special blend of music at yet another talent contest. Tony, managing director of the Castleblayney-based Country Music Management, was so impressed that he immediately arranged for this fresh Country talent to sign a recording deal with his company. Remarkably, considering the fickle nature of the music business, Áine was set and ready to be launched on the national music scene within the space of a few weeks. Her debut single, *I'm Not Lisa*, taken from her Nashville-recorded album of the same name, proved an instant chart hit and was widely regarded as one of the best recordings of 1989 on the Irish market.

Subsequently Áine recorded a second album and also gained significant television exposure while appearing as special guest in the nationwide Search For A Star contest on RTE's popular *Live At Three* programme. Another notable achievement was the fact that Áine appeared alongside many luminaries, including Jerry Lee Lewis, at the 1990 Wembley International Country Music Festival. All that, coupled with a pleasing stage presence, have helped Áine to build up a considerable following on the Irish music circuit.

For singer-guitarist Áine Cromie the best, no doubt, is yet to come.

PROFILE

HOMEPLACE: Killean, County Armagh
BIRTHDAY: August 8
HEIGHT: 5-4
COLOUR OF HAIR: Blonde
COLOUR OF EYES: Blue
ABIDING CHILDHOOD MEMORY: One Christmas Eve night my father dressed up as Santa Claus and was visiting houses in the area. My eldest brother Matthew assured me that it wasn't Santa, it was my father. When he came to our house I said to him, "You're not Santa Claus, you're my daddy". I tried to pull his beard off him but it wouldn't come and I got a big shock. I can tell you, I believed in Santa Claus after that.
EARLY AMBITIONS: To be a singer
FIRST REAL JOB: Lead vocalist with Back Track
EARLIEST RECORDING AND WHEN: I'm Not Lisa, 1989
EARLY MUSICAL INFLUENCES: John Denver, Dolly Parton
HIGHPOINT IN LIFE TO DATE: Recording in Nashville
UNFULFILLED AMBITION: To go to the Olympics and meet all the sports stars
FAVOURITE IRISH ARTISTS: Susan McCann, Daniel O'Donnell
FAVOURITE INTERNATIONAL CELEBRITIES: Dolly Parton, John Denver
FAVOURITE SPORT: Athletics
FAVOURITE FILMS: The Quiet Man, The Blues Brothers
FAVOURITE SONG OR MUSICAL ITEM: The Rose (Elaine Paige)
FAVOURITE NON-SHOWBUSINESS PASTIME: Working out in the gym and going for long walks
WHO WOULD YOU MOST LIKE TO MEET: John Denver
THE QUALITY YOU MOST ADMIRE IN OTHERS: Caring and respect towards others

STAR COMMENT

"There are no stars, only those in the sky and, although the music business seems rosy, along with the roses come the thorns just as in every walk of life. As long as you have your family behind you, you can overcome all obstacles."

B A R L E Y C O R N

Barleycorn are recognised as a first-class trio, much in demand for concert appearances

*T*he popularity of Barleycorn, comprising John Delaney, Derek McCormack and Maurice McCarthy, is not confined to these shores: tours of Australia, Canada, the US and, more recently, New Zealand and Malta are an important part of their itinerary. The Malta visit was arranged specifically to coincide with the Republic of Ireland's World Cup qualifying match in Ta' Quali stadium on 15 November 1989. As everyone knows, Ireland won the match, thereby qualifying for the World Cup Finals. Immediately after that great Irish performance Barleycorn sang many of their hit songs, much to the delight of the Irish fans assembled in the stadium.

The multi-talented group has been in operation since 1970, although the personnel has changed somewhat during the intervening years. John Delaney, who plays guitar, mandolin and banjo, forms the one remaining link with the original line-up and has been involved with many successful recordings issued down the years by Barleycorn, including *Cavan Girl, Portland Town, My Last Farewell* and *Fields of Athenry*, which became a huge hit for the group in 1982, spending seventeen weeks in the Irish charts. Then in 1986 Barleycorn were commissioned to record and produce the music soundtrack for the video, *Isle Of Memories*, which was hugely popular in the US.

Today, Barleycorn are recognised as a first-class trio, much in demand for concert appearances in many parts of the world. *Roisin,* a recent release, was immensely popular and had the distinction of "going platinum" in Australia, where Barleycorn are almost as well known as they are in their native land. Even now, they are planning further concert tours to bring their own special blend of traditional ballad and folk to other farflung destinations.

As the song says, twenty-one years is a mighty long time, but time flies when you're having fun and at the same time working at what gives you most satisfaction, bringing music and song to appreciative audiences.

PROFILE

DEREK McCORMACK: LEAD VOCALIST

HOMEPLACE: Drogheda, County Louth
BIRTHDAY: July 30
HEIGHT: 5-11
COLOUR OF HAIR: Brown
COLOUR OF EYES: Brown
ABIDING CHILDHOOD MEMORY: All of my family were in show business and were involved in the fitups shows. Ours was called the Martin Roadshow, named after my grandfather, Joe Martin. I have many happy memories of singing with them and taking part in the plays.
EARLY AMBITIONS: To be involved in the entertainment business
FIRST REAL JOB: Working in a furniture store
EARLIEST RECORDING AND WHEN: Cavan Girl, 1983
EARLY MUSICAL INFLUENCES: Older members of my family and The Emmet Spiceland
HIGHPOINT IN LIFE TO DATE: Headlining the Australian National Folk Festival
UNFULFILLED AMBITION: To have a number one hit in Ireland
FAVOURITE IRISH ARTISTS: Maura O'Connell, Jim McCann
FAVOURITE INTERNATIONAL CELEBRITIES: Richard Harris, Gordon Lightfoot
FAVOURITE SPORT: Hurling, soccer
FAVOURITE FILMS: Cry Freedom, The Little Drummer Girl
FAVOURITE SONG OR MUSICAL ITEM: Meditation from Thais
FAVOURITE NON-SHOWBUSINESS PASTIME: Playing golf
WHO WOULD YOU MOST LIKE TO MEET: Peter Ustinov
THE QUALITY YOU MOST ADMIRE IN OTHERS: Honesty

STAR COMMENT

"Generally, I would like to see a little more modern thinking in our country."

PHILOMENA BEGLEY

> *Consummate professional who possesses that indefinable magic which is star quality*

*P*hilomena Begley has been right at the very top of Irish show business for close on three decades. Much more than a singer of good songs, Philomena is a symbol of all things positive and enriching in Country and Irish music. There is no doubt that Philomena is a consummate professional who possesses that indefinable magic which is star quality. That she still continues to be hugely popular on the Irish and British music scene is a tribute to her versatility as an entertainer and to her endurance.

There are many reasons why Philomena Begley is more closely associated with Country Music in Ireland than possibly any other female entertainer, perhaps because she has few peers as a live performer. Anyone who has ever watched her perform will attest to the fact that she has total respect for her audience and never fails to put on a quality show.

Philomena Begley's musical journey began as lead vocalist with the Old Cross Ceili Band in the Sixties. Sometime later the band changed its name to Country Flavour and adopted a change of style to Country music. It was an astute move. Within a relatively short period, Philomena enjoyed national success with *Never Again* and *Here Today Gone Tomorrow*, a song which spent nine weeks in the Irish charts. Eventually the Pomeroy, County Tyrone, lady formed her own band, The Ramblin' Men, and with them she recorded some of her best material, much of which made it into the Irish charts: *Ramblin Man, Light In The Window, Wait A Little Longer, Once Around The Dance Floor,* her enduring hit, *Blanket On The Ground* and *Whiskey Drinkin' You,* songs which played a major part in propelling Philomena to stardom.

The former European Gold Star Award winner has also appeared on numerous occasions on the Grand Ole Opry in Nashville, becoming friends with such big-name stars as Tammy Wynette, Hank Snow, Boxcar Willie and Porter Wagoner who, incidentally, has produced many of her best-selling albums.

Philomena's achievements have not gone unnoticed and she has been the recipient of various music awards, including that of Most Popular British Female Vocalist on several occasions. Numerous gold and silver disc awards for outstanding record sales are further testimony to her popularity. It seems that Philomena Begley, entertainer extraordinaire and "Queen Of Country" looks set to reign for many more years to come.

PROFILE

HOMEPLACE: *Pomeroy, County Tyrone*
BIRTHDAY: *October 20*
HEIGHT: *5-4*
COLOUR OF HAIR: *Fair*
COLOUR OF EYES: *Green*
ABIDING CHILDHOOD MEMORY: *Singing a duet with a girl named Mary McConnell in Clarrie Hayden's Travelling Show – best of all, we won ten shillings for it*
EARLY AMBITIONS: *To be a nurse*
FIRST REAL JOB: *Working in Fishers Hat Factory, in Cookstown, County Tyrone*
EARLIEST RECORDING AND WHEN: *My Little Son, 1968*
EARLY MUSICAL INFLUENCES: *Hank Williams*
HIGHPOINT IN LIFE TO DATE: *Winning the European Gold Star Award in Holland in 1983*
UNFULFILLED AMBITION: *To present my very own TV series*
FAVOURITE IRISH ARTISTS: *Tony Stevens, Mary Black*
FAVOURITE INTERNATIONAL CELEBRITIES: *George Jones, Jeannie Pruett*
FAVOURITE SPORT: *Gaelic football*
FAVOURITE FILMS: *The Quiet Man, Crocodile Dundee*
FAVOURITE SONG OR MUSICAL ITEM: *Bridge Over Troubled Waters*
FAVOURITE NON-SHOWBUSINESS PASTIME: *Spending time with my family*
WHO WOULD YOU MOST LIKE TO MEET: *Ian Botham*
THE QUALITY YOU MOST ADMIRE IN OTHERS: *Naturalness*

STAR COMMENT

"Be grateful for the things you have in life."

B I G   T O M

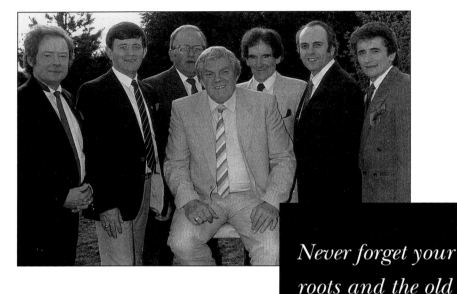

Never forget your roots and the old friends of yesterday

Whenever the greats of Irish show business are being discussed, the name Big Tom is sure to figure prominently. For close on a decade, between the mid-Sixties and Seventies, the legendary "Gentle Giant of Country Music" enjoyed the kind of fan worship now reserved for current superstar, Daniel O'Donnell. During that period, Big Tom's unmistakable voice blended with the authentic sound of The Mainliners to thrill Country music patrons of all ages.

As with many of his contemporaries, one lucky break was all it required to set the Castleblayney singer on the high road to stardom. It happened when The Mainliners were invited to appear on the famous RTE *Showband Show*, and, unexpectedly, Tom had the opportunity to sing *Gentle Mother*. The song provoked such positive reaction that Big Tom was immediately installed as lead vocalist with The Mainliners. Subsequently, Big Tom and The Mainliners became the number one Country attraction at all major dancehall venues, not just in Ireland, but also overseas.

In the intervening years, Big Tom had a succession of hit singles: *Old Log Cabin For Sale, Old Rustic Bridge, Sunset Years Of Life, Back To Castleblayney*, plus three number one hits in the early Seventies, *Broken Marriage Vows, I Love You Still* and *Old Love Letters*.

In 1975, after more than a decade at the peak of his profession, Big Tom accepted the daunting challenge of fronting his own band, The Travellers, and continued to hold his rating as Ireland's most popular Country singer. Meanwhile, John Glenn replaced Big Tom as lead singer with The Mainliners.

Due to public demand Big Tom and The Mainliners re-formed in 1989 for what proved to be an enormously successful tour, and it now seems likely that the revered combination will continue to play together for the foreseeable future.

There is no doubt that Big Tom and The Mainliners have made an immense contribution to the healthy state of Country music in Ireland.

PROFILE

HOMEPLACE: *Moy, Drumakill, Castleblayney, County Monaghan*
BIRTHDAY: *September 18*
HEIGHT: *6.00½*
COLOUR OF HAIR: *Ginger*
COLOUR OF EYES: *Blue/Grey*
ABIDING CHILDHOOD MEMORY: *My last day at school, which I left when I was fourteen, the happiest day I ever had at school; and Sunday mornings when we'd have a feed of sausages, bacon and eggs and it was something I looked forward to all week long*
EARLY AMBITIONS: *To be a carpenter*
FIRST REAL JOB: *Farm hand*
EARLIEST RECORDING AND WHEN: *Gentle Mother, 1966*
EARLY MUSICAL INFLUENCES: *Hank Williams, Porter Wagoner*
HIGHPOINT IN LIFE TO DATE: *Going to the Grand Ole Opry and meeting Stonewall Jackson, Hank Snow and Minnie Pearl, especially Stonewall Jackson as I'd performed many of his songs in the early days*
UNFULFILLED AMBITION: *None really. I'm very happy with the way things are at the moment. I would like to catch a big fish, though, one I wouldn't have to tell a lie about.*
FAVOURITE IRISH ARTISTS: *Margo, Brian Coll*
FAVOURITE INTERNATIONAL CELEBRITIES: *Princess Diana, Barry McGuigan*
FAVOURITE SPORT: *Gaelic football*
FAVOURITE FILMS: *Your Cheatin' Heart, Shane*
FAVOURITE SONG OR MUSICAL ITEM: *Gentle Mother*
FAVOURITE NON-SHOWBUSINESS PASTIME: *Fishing, snooker.*
WHO WOULD YOU MOST LIKE TO MEET: *Mick Jagger*
THE QUALITY YOU MOST ADMIRE IN OTHERS: *Sincerity*

STAR COMMENT

"Never forget your roots and the old friends of yesterday. No matter how successful you are it's important to remember where you came from."

BRENDAN BOWYER

The Hucklebuck captured precisely the mood of the Swinging Sixties in Ireland

*B*rendan Bowyer is among Ireland's most popular and enduring entertainers.

Before turning full-time professional Brendan worked for the National Board and Paper Mills in his native Waterford city and, while there, he befriended another employee, Tom Dunphy, now sadly deceased. Impressed with young Brendan's potential as a vocalist, Tom convinced him that his future lay in a show business career. A short time later in 1959 the two friends became part of the newly formed Royal Showband. Those who knew him well were delighted with Brendan's change of career as he belonged to a family with a rich musical tradition. His grandparents owned The Bowyer Westwood Opera Company and his mother was an accomplished opera singer.

Within a short period The Royal Showband had become a major attraction at dancehall venues all over Ireland. Not surprisingly, they had a succession of chart hits, including *Kiss Me Quick* (seven weeks at number one), *No More* and *Bless You*. Brendan also won the prestigious Carl Allan Award from the British music industry in 1962 and, as a result, received considerable exposure on BBC television. But it was his recording of an old song called *The Hucklebuck* that may be said to have launched Brendan on the road to lasting stardom. A highly infectious song, it remained at the top of the Irish charts for seven weeks and, more than any other recording of the time, captured precisely the mood of the Swinging Sixties in Ireland. Moreover, it remains as popular today as when it was first recorded over a quarter of a century ago.

In the early Seventies Brendan became aware of a steady decline in the Irish music business and decided to move to Las Vegas with his new band, The Big 8, where they established themselves in major resort hotels. Brendan has been resident there since then, making occasional visits home by popular demand, much to the delight of his fans, old and new.

Some may come and some may go, but one thing remains certain: Brendan Bowyer, like his great song, *The Hucklebuck*, will continue to be a firm favourite with Irish music lovers for many years to come.

PROFILE

HOMEPLACE: Waterford City
BIRTHDAY: October 12
HEIGHT: 6-2 ½
COLOUR OF HAIR: Black
COLOUR OF EYES: Green
ABIDING CHILDHOOD MEMORY: Visiting opera and variety companies;
also the impact of the birth of Rock and Roll in the Fifties
EARLY AMBITIONS: To have a career in classical music
FIRST REAL JOB: A sales clerk with the National Board and Paper Mills
in Waterford
EARLIEST RECORDING AND WHEN: Kiss Me Quick, 1963
EARLY MUSICAL INFLUENCES: Classical from my father and mother
HIGHPOINT IN LIFE TO DATE: The phenomenal extended success of
The Royal Showband – so many peaks and so few valleys
UNFULFILLED AMBITION: A definitive recording to be remembered by
FAVOURITE IRISH ARTISTS: Joe Dolan, Dickie Rock, Mary Black
FAVOURITE INTERNATIONAL CELEBRITIES: Jimmy Connors,
Jack Nicklaus
FAVOURITE SPORT: Hard to mention only one: hurling
FAVOURITE FILMS: Chariots Of Fire, Dr Zhivago, Goodbye Mr Chips
(1939 original)
FAVOURITE SONG OR MUSICAL ITEM: Smoke Gets In Your Eyes (Platters)
FAVOURITE NON-SHOWBUSINESS PASTIMES: Travelling to new places,
good movies
WHO WOULD YOU MOST LIKE TO MEET: Pope John Paul II
THE QUALITY YOU MOST ADMIRE IN OTHERS: Sincerity and consistency

STAR COMMENT

"I feel so sad to have wasted so many of the middle years, but feel blessed to have survived and gone from strength to strength in the autumn years."

A N N B R E E N

There was never a time when music wasn't part of Ann Breen's life

*A*nn Breen, "The Star Of The County Down", first came to national prominence in 1981 with a hugely popular song called *Pal Of My Cradle Days*. Taken from her album of the same name, it remained in the lower regions of the British charts for over two years, earning the Downpatrick singer a gold disc award and a place in The Guinness Book Of Song Records.

Subsequently Ann signed a contract with Noel Carty, manager of Brendan Shine and Johnny McEvoy, and thereafter her career flourished beyond expectations. Ann formed her own band in 1983 and her crystal-clear singing voice and impressive stage performances soon endeared her to music patrons of all ages.

It seems there was never a time when music wasn't part of Ann Breen's life and she vividly recalls both her grandmothers, Elizabeth and Annie, singing all the old Delia Murphy, Doris Day, Vera Lynn and Ruby Murray favourites. While at primary school in the Convent of Mercy, Downpatrick, Ann continued her interest in singing by joining the school and church choirs. Later, as a student in the Assumption Grammar School, Ballynahinch, Ann took part in all the operettas and in her final year there she played the lead role in *The Gypsy Baron*.

Since turning professional, the soft-spoken lady of Country and Irish has had the honour of representing Ireland in both the European Gold Star Awards final and the Golden Harp Country Music Festival. Another noteworthy achievement was the fact that her recording of the Ron McWilliams song, *Love Is*, was used by Kim Casali to promote her internationally renowned product of the same name.

Over the years Ann Breen has built up a considerable reputation from her regular appearances on various television networks, including RTE, UTV, Granada and BBC, and she gained considerable experience from appearing as special guest on the Brendan Shine Annual UK Concert tours. Nowadays, though, Ann Breen is recognised as a headline star in her own right, fronting concerts throughout England, Scotland and Wales.

Ann Breen will always command a special place in the hearts of Irish music lovers.

PROFILE

HOMEPLACE: Downpatrick, County Down
BIRTHDAY: January 8
HEIGHT: 5-4
COLOUR OF HAIR: Medium Brown
COLOUR OF EYES: Grey/Green
ABIDING CHILDHOOD MEMORY: Singing Edelweiss in the Canon's Hall in Downpatrick and coming first in my category; I was only nine years old at the time
EARLY AMBITIONS: To be a singer
FIRST REAL JOB: Secretary to the Principal in the Assumption Convent School, Ballynahinch, County Down
EARLIEST RECORDING AND WHEN: Country Songbird album, 1981
EARLY MUSICAL INFLUENCES: Listening to both my grandmothers, Elizabeth and Annie, singing the songs of Bridie Gallagher, Vera Lynn, Eileen Donaghy, Doris Day and, of course, Delia Murphy
HIGHPOINT IN LIFE TO DATE: Receiving a gold disc award for Pal Of My Cradle Days
UNFULFILLED AMBITION: To play a starring role in a hit musical
FAVOURITE IRISH ARTISTS: Brendan Bowyer, Ruby Murray
FAVOURITE INTERNATIONAL CELEBRITIES: Dolly Parton, Kenny Rogers
FAVOURITE SPORT: Athletics
FAVOURITE FILMS: Beaches, One Flew Over The Cuckoo's Nest
FAVOURITE SONG OR MUSICAL ITEM: Que Sera Sera
FAVOURITE NON-SHOWBUSINESS PASTIME: Reading novels
WHO WOULD YOU MOST LIKE TO MEET: Pope John Paul II
THE QUALITY YOU MOST ADMIRE IN OTHERS: Honesty

STAR COMMENT

"Live every day to the full and enjoy it."

THE CAPITOL SHOWBAND

In 1965 Butch Moore represented Ireland in the Eurovision Song Contest

*I*t is many years since The Capitol Showband last played together as a unit, yet they will forever be remembered as one of the most loved and respected combinations ever to grace the Irish music scene.

It was as college students in the late Fifties that Eamonn Monaghan, Paul Sweeney, Des Kelly and Johnny Kelly, now sadly deceased, came up with the idea of forming a band. The following summer while holidaying in Galway they began to attract considerable attention with their own lively brand of music and persevered to go into the business professionally. The next step was to find some more talented singers and musicians to join them. The search uncovered such emerging talents as Jimmy Hogan, Butch Moore, Paddy Cole and Don Long, each of them a gifted entertainer. About a year later, Paul Sweeney left to further his education and was replaced by trumpeter Bram McCarthy.

Not surprisingly, considering their abundant talent, The Capitol built up a hugely loyal following in Ireland and England. Their own series, *The Capitol Showband Show,* on Radio Luxembourg enhanced their growing reputations, as did appearances on major television shows, including *Sunday*

Night At The Palladium, Count Your Lucky Stars and the *Eamonn Andrews Show*. In 1964 The Capitol had their first chart hit, *Foolin' Time,* and this was followed by superb versions of *Down Came The Rain* and *Born To Be With You,* both of which raced to the top of the Irish charts.

At that stage they could do no wrong, and in 1965 Butch Moore represented Ireland in the Eurovision Song Contest in Naples with *Walking The Streets In The Rain.* The band were mobbed on their return to Dublin and were seen as veritable superstars on the Irish music scene.

In the late Sixties Butch Moore left to pursue a solo career but The Capitol still continued to perform to appreciative audiences until 1970, when they decided to go their separate ways, truly marking the end of a glorious era in Irish show business.

However, for those privileged to have seen The Capitol, memories linger of days when the showbands ruled and the whole world seemed young.

PROFILE

PADDY COLE

HOMEPLACE: *Castleblayney, County Monaghan*
BIRTHDAY: *December 17*
HEIGHT: *6-01½*
COLOUR OF HAIR: *Used to be black*
COLOUR OF EYES: *Blueish*
ABIDING CHILDHOOD MEMORY: *My father playing the saxophone*
EARLY AMBITIONS: *To be in a top band*
FIRST REAL JOB: *I've always been a musician*
EARLIEST RECORDING AND WHEN: *Capitol album in the early Sixties*
EARLY MUSICAL INFLUENCES: *My father*
HIGHPOINT IN LIFE TO DATE: *Seeing my son Pearse graduate from Trinity College*
UNFULFILLED AMBITION: *To graduate from Trinity College*
FAVOURITE IRISH ARTISTS: *Matt Molloy, Twink*
FAVOURITE INTERNATIONAL CELEBRITIES: *Jack Nicholson, Colm Wilkinson*
FAVOURITE SPORT: *Gaelic football*
FAVOURITE FILMS: *The Blues Brothers, The Godfather*
FAVOURITE SONG OR MUSICAL ITEM: *MacArthur Park*
FAVOURITE NON-SHOWBUSINESS PASTIME: *Golf and fishing*
WHO WOULD YOU MOST LIKE TO MEET: *President Gorbachev*
THE QUALITY YOU MOST ADMIRE IN OTHERS: *Tenacity*

STAR COMMENT

"I think we've got to be very aware of the pollution of our lakes and rivers. Being a guy who loves to fish, I hate to hear of a fish kill resulting from negligence in industry or farming. We have a duty to protect our lakes and rivers for future generations of Irish people and visitors."

DOC CARROLL

Now you're talking show business

*T*he name Martin O'Carroll would mean nothing to Irish music followers; but, change the Christian name to Doc, delete the O', add a song, preferably *Old Man Trouble*, then complete the picture with a touch of royal blue and now you're talking show business, the Sixties, showbands and real musical magic: Doc Carroll and The Royal Blues. Who else?

The son of a doctor, from Tourmakeady, County Mayo, Martin was given the nickname, Doc, by Brother Helian, his teacher at the CBS in Ballinrobe. He was barely five years old at the time, but the new name caught on immediately and has served him well in his chosen profession.

His very earliest introduction to professional life came about when Doc, all of sixteen years of age, spent two weeks in England with Sligo-based band, The Clefonaires. A year later he left Atlantic College, where he was training to be a radio officer, and teamed up with the Kiltimagh-based Pete Brown Band, and it was four of its members, Frank Gill, Vincent Gill, Brian Carr and Doc, who formed the nucleus of The Royal Blues, and turned semi-professional in November 1962, under the management of Andy Creighton. Four Dublin musicians, Shay O'Hara, Don Flanagan, Bobby Smith and Brendan Arnold, completed the line-up. Such was the positive reaction that the following May in the Five Counties Ballroom, Toreen,

County Mayo, The Royal Blues were launched as full-time professionals. Soon the fledgling outfit, with Shay O'Hara as lead vocalist, had become one of the major dance-band attractions in the West of Ireland. At that time Doc Carroll was the band's lead guitar player, but when it was decided he should record *Old Man Trouble* The Royal Blues became national stars. Doc's version of the old Fats Domino number raced to the top of the Irish charts, and to this very day *Old Man Trouble* is the song most people identify with The Royal Blues.

During the height of their popularity The Royal Blues undertook many extensive tours of Great Britain and the US, where they appeared in Carnegie Hall, New York and CBS television in the same city.

The Royal Blues have not played together as a professional unit since 1972, but Doc, whose anniversary celebration of twenty-five years in show business was hosted by BBC personality Terry Wogan, has played with a number of musical combinations including The Nightrunners and he continues to sing his songs with all the aplomb of the master craftsman that he is.

PROFILE

HOMEPLACE: *Tourmakeady, County Mayo*
BIRTHDAY: *November 19*
HEIGHT: *5-8*
COLOUR OF HAIR: *Brown*
COLOUR OF EYES: *Blue*
ABIDING CHILDHOOD MEMORY: *Seeing planes landing in Shannon at night time. When I was nine my eldest brother was emigrating to the US and all the family travelled to Shannon Airport to see him off. I'll never forget the excitement of watching the aircraft and hearing the drone of the engines.*
EARLY AMBITIONS: *To travel to the US*
FIRST REAL JOB: *Musician*
EARLIEST RECORDING AND WHEN: *Old Man Trouble, 1966*
EARLY MUSICAL INFLUENCES: *Elvis, Fats Domino*
HIGHPOINT IN LIFE TO DATE: *Reaching number one in the Irish charts with Old Man Trouble in 1966*
UNFULFILLED AMBITION: *To have a hit in the British charts*
FAVOURITE IRISH ARTISTS: *Seamus Shannon, Dolores Keane*
FAVOURITE INTERNATIONAL CELEBRITIES: *George Best, Candice Bergin*
FAVOURITE SPORT: *All sports, but especially gaelic football and soccer*
FAVOURITE FILMS: *The Magnificent Seven, Dirty Dozen*
FAVOURITE SONG OR MUSICAL ITEM: *Blueberry Hill*
FAVOURITE NON-SHOWBUSINESS PASTIME: *Fishing*
WHO WOULD YOU MOST LIKE TO MEET: *Abba*
THE QUALITY YOU MOST ADMIRE IN OTHERS: *Compassion*

STAR COMMENT

"The worst thing that has befallen the human race is greed and, unfortunately, we learn that when sickness comes and sadness looms."

JOHNNY CARROLL

After thirty years in the music business, Johnny Carroll still shows no sign of cutting

*A*nyone who has ever watched him perform will be aware that Johnny Carroll is a gifted entertainer. During the past few years his excellent trumpet playing, combined with a thoroughly professional stage show, has proved a winning formula with Irish music fans.

A native of County Roscommon now living in Galway, Johnny claims to be one of the very few Irish entertainers to have made show business his full-time profession since childhood. In the early Sixties at the tender age of thirteen, Johnny teamed up with The Premier Aces Showband, noted for the fact that all of the members were teetotal. He was then Ireland's youngest professional musician. Johnny remained with the Premier Aces for thirteen years before leaving with some of the other band members to form Murphy and The Swallows. Later he teamed up with Magic and The Magic Band, a novelty dance-band who created quite a stir because their lead vocalist wore a lighted suit.

Then in the early Eighties, in an attempt to overcome the dramatic fall-off in the number of patrons attending live shows, Johnny decided on a change of style and since then, with the emphasis very much on his trumpet playing, he has gradually gained a wider audience. Johnny had cause for celebration when he received a gold disc award for sales of his debut album, *Touch Of Class*, and he was accorded similar accolades for both his follow-up album, *Golden Moments*, and his most recently released compilation, *From The Heart*.

Johnny, who got the now famous tag, "The Man With The Golden Trumpet", as a result of featuring much of Eddie Calvert's music in his repertoire, is also very proud of the fact that he's the only Irish trumpeter to have reached a top three position in the charts with an instrumental number, *O Mein Papa*. Now, after thirty years in the music business, Johnny Carroll still shows no sign of cutting back on his heavy schedule and remains eager as ever to ply his trade. All of which is good news for his legion of followers.

PROFILE

HOMEPLACE: *Castlerea, County Roscommon*
BIRTHDAY: *October 24*
HEIGHT: *5-8*
COLOUR OF HAIR: *Ginger*
COLOUR OF EYES: *Blue*
ABIDING CHILDHOOD MEMORY: *Standing, as a young boy in short trousers, outside the Savoy Ballroom in Castlerea listening to the bands playing inside*
EARLY AMBITIONS: *To be a musician*
FIRST REAL JOB: *Musician*
EARLIEST RECORDING AND WHEN: *Above And Beyond with Houston Wells and The Premier Aces, 1965*
EARLY MUSICAL INFLUENCES: *Trumpeter Eddie Calvert*
HIGHPOINT IN LIFE TO DATE: *Playing in Croke Park during the half-time interval at the 1988 All-Ireland Hurling Final before 65,000 people and a worldwide audience of millions*
UNFULFILLED AMBITION: *To have an international hit*
FAVOURITE IRISH ARTISTS: *Tony Stevens, Sandy Kelly*
FAVOURITE INTERNATIONAL CELEBRITIES: *Herb Alpert, James Last*
FAVOURITE SPORT: *Soccer*
FAVOURITE FILMS: *The Quiet Man, Shane*
FAVOURITE SONG OR MUSICAL ITEM: *O Mein Papa*
FAVOURITE NON-SHOWBUSINESS PASTIME: *Relaxing at home with my family*
WHO WOULD YOU MOST LIKE TO MEET: *Nelson Mandela*
THE QUALITY YOU MOST ADMIRE IN OTHERS: *Sincerity*

STAR COMMENT

"I would love to see peace in our country and the Irish people living as one."

NOEL CASSIDY

> *Noel feels a great affinity for the many Irish who are forced to emigrate*

*T*he Country music revival and the increasing success of a whole array of newcomers convinced Noel Cassidy that he should follow the popular trend and try his hand at recording Country and Irish material. Previously, Noel had confined his musical activities to frequent appearances on the local pub and cabaret scene in his native County Longford.

In the very early seventies Noel Cassidy took the emigrant boat. He was no more than fifteen at the time. Indeed, because of his early introduction to life away from home, Noel now feels a great affinity for the many Irish who are forced to emigrate. While in Britain Noel developed a keen interest in music, and before returning to Ireland he purchased a guitar. Subsequently he formed a group called the Wagonmasters and built up a steady following in the Longford and surrounding areas. When the time came to turn professional, Noel was well and truly ready, not simply eager.

Noel's debut ten-track cassette, containing such standards as *You Seldom Come To See Me Anymore, Rose Of The Mountain, Lusmagh Fields* and *The Moods Of Mary,* proved especially popular, particularly around the Midlands. His first four-track cassette/EP release, *We'll Sweep Out The Ashes In The Morning,* received a good degree of airplay on national and regional radio. In 1990 his recording of *Southern Dixie Flyer*, a four-track cassette/EP, marked Noel Cassidy's coming of age in the Country music world. Apart from the title track, Noel featured a selection of American and Irish material, including *Railroad Bum, Old Love Letters* and *My Grass is Greener*. The compilation fully deserved the success it earned and proved a worthwhile investment. Furthermore, his marvellous follow-up release, *Old Time Waltz*, written specifically for Noel by Peter Lawlor, a former member of The Pacific, did much to enhance the Ballinamuck's singer's reputation as a recording artist.

These days Noel is in constant demand, thanks to his relaxed stage presence and lively musical repertoire.

It is never easy to secure that all-important breakthrough but Noel Cassidy has shown that he possesses the requisite talent and commitment.

PROFILE

HOMEPLACE: *Ballinamuck, County Longford*
BIRTHDAY: *December 31*
HEIGHT: *5-9*
COLOUR OF HAIR: *Black*
COLOUR OF EYES: *Brown*
ABIDING CHILDHOOD MEMORY: *Hearing the newsflash of the assassination of President John F. Kennedy on RTE. Even though I was only eight at the time it's something I'll never forget.*
EARLY AMBITIONS: *To be a musician*
FIRST REAL JOB: *Machine driver*
EARLIEST RECORDING AND WHEN: *Souvenirs Album of Country and Irish, 1987*
EARLY MUSICAL INFLUENCES: *Buck Owens, Big Tom*
HIGHPOINT IN LIFE TO DATE: *Appearing in front of 80,000 people at the London Irish Festival in Roundwood Park*
UNFULFILLED AMBITION: *To have a number one hit*
FAVOURITE IRISH ARTISTS: *Big Tom, Philomena Begley*
FAVOURITE INTERNATIONAL CELEBRITIES: *Buck Owens, Dolly Parton*
FAVOURITE SPORT: *Gaelic football*
FAVOURITE FILMS: *Hard Country, The Quiet Man*
FAVOURITE SONG OR MUSICAL ITEM: *My Way by Elvis*
FAVOURITE NON-SHOWBUSINESS PASTIME: *Working on the farm*
WHO WOULD YOU MOST LIKE TO MEET: *Pope John Paul II*
THE QUALITY YOU MOST ADMIRE IN OTHERS: *Trustworthiness*

STAR COMMENT

"Don't let life get you down."

CHUCK AND JUNE

Two of the most talented performers on the Irish music circuit

*C*huck and June Owens, regarded by many as two of the most talented performers on the Irish music circuit, are the extremely popular husband and wife singing duo who front the Midlands-based band, The Gamblers.

Chuck was born in Granard, County Longford, and began his musical career playing the local pub circuit, while June, a native of Derry City, entered the business more by accident than design. It seems that while attending a bingo session in the local hall she was encouraged by her father to take the stage when the person who usually entertained the patrons during intermissions failed to appear. That was the beginning of what has, so far, been a rewarding and fruitful career. Although probably no more than fourteen at the time, June impressed the organisers so much that she was invited back to perform on a weekly basis. (Incidentally, those bingo sessions were organised by Father Daly, who is now Bishop of Derry.)

Chuck had an early introduction to the music scene and remembers playing the accordion at the Fleadh Cheoil in Granard when barely seven years old. By the time Chuck had reached the age of nine he was taking lessons on the violin but when his older brother, Hughie, purchased a guitar Chuck had found his vocation. While still at national school Chuck joined the family band, The Swinging Stars, and remained with them for about four years, during which time they had a residency in the Irish Centre, Swindon. When he returned from England, Chuck recorded his first song, *Jeannie's Afraid Of The Dark*, and secured the position of lead singer with the Wagon Wheels. Those were exciting times for a singer/ musician and Chuck enjoyed every minute of it. Subsequently, Chuck played with a number of musical combinations, including The Sahara Showband, The Navac Showband, The Everglades and The Smokies.

Although June became a trainee nurse at sixteen, she still found time to guest as a singer at various charity shows. Later she sang with a local group in the Squealing Pig bar in Muff, County Donegal, and from there June progressed to fronting a local band, The Silver Sands, then teamed up with Frank Chisum and The Top Seven, before eventually fronting The Smokies with future husband, Chuck. Consequently, they were approached by a music promoter with a view to backing Larry Cunningham who, at the time, was in the process of forming a new band. There followed six very enjoyable years during which time June and Larry recorded a duet called *Don't Let Me Cross Over*. Considering their natural musical talent, it was no surprise that Chuck and June eventually decided to form The Gamblers, a band now noted for its authentic Country sound.

Very successful on the ballroom and cabaret circuit, particularly in Britain, Chuck, June and The Gamblers are thoroughly enjoying their well-earned spell in the limelight.

PROFILE

CHUCK

HOMEPLACE: Granard, County Longford
BIRTHDAY: August 7
HEIGHT: 5-8
COLOUR OF HAIR: Fair
COLOUR OF EYES: Blue
ABIDING CHILDHOOD MEMORY: Going to hear all the bands in the Granada Ballroom, Granard
EARLY AMBITIONS: To play steel guitar
FIRST REAL JOB: Builder
EARLIEST RECORDING AND WHEN: Jeannie's Afraid Of The Dark, 1971
EARLY MUSICAL INFLUENCES: George Jones
HIGHPOINT IN LIFE TO DATE: Appearing at the Wembley International Country Music Festival
UNFULFILLED AMBITION: To have a hit record
FAVOURITE IRISH ARTISTS: Ray Lynam, Susan McCann
FAVOURITE INTERNATIONAL CELEBRITIES: George Jones, Dolly Parton
FAVOURITE SPORT: Darts

FAVOURITE FILMS: Any Marx Brothers films
FAVOURITE SONG OR MUSICAL ITEM: Forever And Ever Amen
FAVOURITE NON-SHOWBUSINESS PASTIME: Relaxing and having a
drink with my friends
WHO WOULD YOU MOST LIKE TO MEET: Dolly Parton
THE QUALITY YOU MOST ADMIRE IN OTHERS: Reliability

STAR COMMENT

"Don't allow success go to your head."

PROFILE

JUNE

HOMEPLACE: Derry City
BIRTHDAY: August 8
HEIGHT: 5-3
COLOUR OF HAIR: Dark Brown
COLOUR OF EYES: Green
ABIDING CHILDHOOD MEMORY: Going to the pictures in the
Rialto Cinema, Derry, with my father
EARLY AMBITIONS: To be a nurse
FIRST REAL JOB: Nursing
EARLIEST RECORDING AND WHEN: One Day At A Time, 1974
EARLY MUSICAL INFLUENCES: Joseph Locke, Eileen Donaghy
HIGHPOINT IN LIFE TO DATE: Appearing at the Wembley International
Country Music Festival
UNFULFILLED AMBITION: To sing in Nashville
FAVOURITE IRISH ARTISTS: Louise Morrissey, Brian Coll
FAVOURITE INTERNATIONAL CELEBRITIES: Kathy Mathea, George Jones
FAVOURITE SPORT: Snooker
FAVOURITE FILMS: My Left Foot, The Untouchables
FAVOURITE SONG OR MUSICAL ITEM: The Town I Loved So Well
FAVOURITE NON-SHOWBUSINESS PASTIME: Watching videos and
listening to records
WHO WOULD YOU MOST LIKE TO MEET: Mel Gibson
THE QUALITY YOU MOST ADMIRE IN OTHERS: Honesty

STAR COMMENT

"No matter how successful you are, always remember those who helped put you there."

THE CLANCY BROTHERS & TOMMY MAKEM

They sold out major concert halls all over the world

*T*he Clancy Brothers and Tommy Makem are an Irish institution. Indeed, it is fair to say that there was a time in the 1960s when they were Ireland's best-known and most popular musical ambassadors. Pat, Tom and Liam Clancy were born in Carrick-on-Suir, County Tipperary while Tommy Makem comes from Keady, County Armagh. Their early influences were in theatre, and entry into the top flight of show business came more by accident than design. The lads were booked to perform two songs on the famous Ed Sullivan Show in the US, and when one of the other acts cancelled, the producer of the show asked them to do some extra numbers. And so, without benefit of rehearsal The Clancy Brothers and Tommy Makem played to an audience of over eighty million people. It marked the beginning of a musical legend.

Through the Sixties, the Clancy Brothers and Tommy Makem featured on all the top entertainment shows in Ireland and America. They made more than forty best-selling albums and sold out major concert halls all over the world. Sadly, after more than a decade at the top, they decided to go their separate ways. Audiences still yearned for more of the same but the foursome were in agreement that nothing further could be achieved. Tommy Makem was interested in writing and performing his songs; Liam, also keen on the idea of solo work, headed for Canada, where he presented his own television series; Tom, now sadly deceased, returned to the stage and Pat did the sensible thing and settled for a quiet life on the farm.

All was not lost, however, and such was the positive response when Tommy and Liam performed together at The Cleveland Festival in the mid-Seventies that they decided to renew their partnership as a duo. It was the beginning of a new era. Soon they were putting together best-selling albums and reached number one in the Irish charts with a powerful version of *Waltzing Matilda*.

The Clancy Brothers and Tommy Makem will always be remembered as one of the very first Irish acts to become major international stars. As such their reputation is secure and continues to grow as they and their families are intent on keeping alive that great musical tradition.

PROFILE

LIAM CLANCY

HOMEPLACE: *Carrick-on-Suir, County Tipperary*
BIRTHDAY: *September 2*
HEIGHT: *5-10*
COLOUR OF HAIR: *Brown*
COLOUR OF EYES: *Hazel*
ABIDING CHILDHOOD MEMORY: *Climbing Comeragh Mountains*
EARLY AMBITIONS: *To be an actor and film maker*
FIRST REAL JOB: *Insurance clerk*
EARLIEST RECORDING AND WHEN: *Lark In The Morning, 1956*
EARLY MUSICAL INFLUENCES: *Family tradition, Burl Ives, Ewan McColl,*
Josh White
HIGHPOINT IN LIFE: *Presenting Yeats plays with Frank O'Connor in New York*
UNFULFILLED AMBITION: *To write the book I'd be happy with*
FAVOURITE IRISH ARTISTS: *Christy Moore, Michael Coady, Pauline Bewick*
FAVOURITE INTERNATIONAL CELEBRITIES: *Jacques Cousteau, President*
Gorbachev, Mother Teresa
FAVOURITE SPORT: *Scuba diving*
FAVOURITE FILMS: *All John Houston's*
FAVOURITE SONG OR MUSICAL ITEM: *Vincent (Don McClean),*
Three Penny Opera (Brecht)
FAVOURITE NON-SHOWBUSINESS PASTIME: *Nature Studies*
WHO WOULD YOU MOST LIKE TO MEET: *Robert Burns*
THE QUALITY YOU MOST ADMIRE IN OTHERS: *Trustworthiness*

STAR COMMENT

"*Nikos Kazantzakis wrote: 'Each man must consider himself solely responsible for the salvation of the world, because when a man dies, that aspect of the Universe which is his own particular vision and the unique plan of his mind also crashes in ruins forever.'* "

B R I A N   C O L L

> *Ireland has never produced another singer to compare with Count John McCormack*

*B*rian Coll, one of Ireland's most popular singers, feels he is lucky just to be alive and able to sing. In the autumn of 1989 Brian suffered a severe brain haemorrhage which necessitated a lengthy stay in hospital and kept him off the road for over six months. But now he is back and bringing his own special blend of Country and Irish magic to audiences all over Ireland and the UK.

For over three decades the name Brian Coll has been closely identified with pure Country music. It is no surprise then to learn that, as well as being loved and respected by music patrons, the genial singer is also held in high esteem by his fellow-professionals.

Those who know him well will attest to the fact that he is much more than a singer of Country songs. Like his uncle, broadcaster and novelist Dr Benedict Kiely, Brian is a natural storyteller with an assortment of stories to thrill connoisseurs. He himself believes that Ireland has never produced another singer to compare with Count John McCormack and he will tell you that he was strongly influenced by the great tenor.

Growing up in Omagh, County Tyrone, Brian, noted as one of the very few outstanding exponents of yodelling, began his musical career as lead vocalist with The Polka Dots. He also had spells with The Plattermen before forming his own band, The Buckaroos, in 1968. There followed a stream of hit singles: *Give An Irish Girl To Me, These Are My Mountains* (one of the biggest-selling Irish singles), *When My Blue Moon Turns To Gold* and *Home Town On The Foyle*, which earned Brian a nine-week stay in the Irish charts.

Country singer, entertainer and storyteller, but above all an inspirational figure in the world of Country and Irish, Brian Coll, 1989 Country & Irish RTE Guide Hall Of Fame award winner, still gets immense satisfaction from playing to live audiences.

Long may he continue to sing his Country songs.

PROFILE

HOMEPLACE: *Omagh, County Tyrone*
BIRTHDAY: *March 6*
HEIGHT: *6-1*
COLOUR OF HAIR: *Dark Brown*
COLOUR OF EYES: *Green*
ABIDING CHILDHOOD MEMORY: *Watching the local blacksmith,*
Darky Hamilton, shoeing horses
EARLY AMBITIONS: *To be a tenor*
FIRST REAL JOB: *Baker*
EARLIEST RECORDING AND WHEN: *Kathleen, recorded with the*
Plattermen in 1965
EARLY MUSICAL INFLUENCES: *Count John McCormack*
HIGHPOINT IN LIFE TO DATE: *My first daughter Kathy's successful*
heart operation
UNFULFILLED AMBITION: *To write a hit song*
FAVOURITE IRISH ARTISTS: *Hard to say, as I admire so many of them*
FAVOURITE INTERNATIONAL CELEBRITIES: *Mike Hailwood (now deceased),*
Joey Dunlop
FAVOURITE SPORT: *Motorcycle racing*
FAVOURITE FILMS: *The Quiet Man, Gun Fight At The OK Corral*
FAVOURITE SONG OR MUSICAL ITEM: *Kathleen Mavourneen*
FAVOURITE NON-SHOWBUSINESS PASTIME: *Photography*
WHO WOULD YOU MOST LIKE TO MEET: *Pope John Paul II*
THE QUALITY YOU MOST ADMIRE IN OTHERS: *Honesty and good manners*

STAR COMMENT

"I would like to see peace in the world."

J O E   C U D D Y

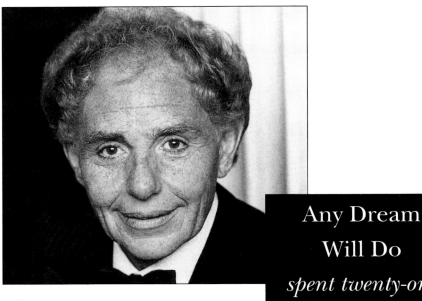

Any Dream Will Do *spent twenty-one weeks in the Irish charts*

Joe Cuddy is often referred to as "Mr Cabaret", and rightly so. Truly the all-round entertainer, Joe possesses a rich strong voice and can tell a story with the precision and timing of a great comedian. Indeed, in 1976 while performing in Arizona, Joe, master of the wisecrack, was applauded by the legendary Bob Hope.

A Dublin man and proud of it, Joe Cuddy began his musical career as a boy soprano, winning prizes at many Feis Ceoil events. In 1966 he launched his cabaret career at the Grand Hotel, Malahide.

Interestingly, his first composition – a guitar instrumental – was recorded by the Hoot' nannys before Joe himself earned chart success in 1972 with *Sticks and Stones*, a song he co-wrote with his sister Eileen. The following year Joe was back in the Irish charts with his winning Castlebar entry, *I'm Gonna Make It*, written by Vince Hill. All that paled into insignificance, however, when Joe released his masterpiece, *Any Dream Will Do*, a song which spent twenty-one weeks in the Irish charts, including two at number one. Suddenly Joe Cuddy's career took flight. In fact, the song made such an impact that it overshadowed many of his other achievements.

Through the years Joe has performed with distinction at various song contests throughout Europe, claiming the top prize in Yugoslavia and also winning Hughie Green's *Opportunity Knocks*. No stranger to television, Joe presented his own RTE series and once co-hosted a one-hour special in Poland.

Nowadays Joe regularly performs abroad for companies and is rated one of the best after-dinner entertainers in the business. Nor does he entertain any thoughts of retiring. Quoting John Wayne, he says, "I'll keep doing it till I get it right".

PROFILE

HOMEPLACE: Raheny, Dublin
BIRTHDAY: March 4
HEIGHT: 5-7
COLOUR OF HAIR: Brown
COLOUR OF EYES: Hazel
ABIDING CHILDHOOD MEMORY: Reading Curley Wee and Gussy Goose annuals
EARLY AMBITIONS: To be a singer
FIRST REAL JOB: Butcher
EARLIEST RECORDING AND WHEN: Sticks and Stones, 1970
EARLY MUSICAL INFLUENCES: Feis Cheoil pieces, jazz
HIGHPOINT IN LIFE TO DATE: My first number one hit
UNFULFILLED AMBITION: To play golf off a scratch handicap
FAVOURITE IRISH ARTISTS: Colm Wilkinson, Maureen Potter
FAVOURITE INTERNATIONAL CELEBRITIES: Frank Sinatra, Neil Diamond
FAVOURITE SPORT: Golf
FAVOURITE FILMS: The Deerhunter, West Side Story
FAVOURITE SONG OR MUSICAL ITEM: Evening Chimes (sung by Ivan Rebroff)
FAVOURITE NON-SHOWBUSINESS PASTIME: Gardening
WHO WOULD YOU MOST LIKE TO MEET: Pope John Paul II
THE QUALITY YOU MOST ADMIRE IN OTHERS: Honesty

STAR COMMENT

"It's very nice to be important, but it is most important to be very nice."

SHAWN CUDDY

Being a singer or entertainer shouldn't make you any different

Shawn Cuddy was born the eldest of eleven in Camross, County Laois. His mother used to purchase all the popular Irish records, and as a result the young Shawn learned at an early age to appreciate the vocal skills of the likes of Margo, Big Tom and Philomena Begley.

During his schooldays, first at Camross National School and later as a boarder in Ballyfin Secondary School, Shawn developed an intense interest in all things musical. He took part in various competitions, both as a solo artist and as part of the Cuddy Family Group, comprising his sisters, Elizabeth, Martina, Linda, Sharon and Fiona.

In 1981, on the advice of Paddy Delaney, a family friend, Shawn formed a three-piece Country band in association with two of his sisters, Elizabeth and Martina. There followed a very rewarding period during which the family group built up a considerable reputation as first-rate entertainers.

When his sisters left the group, Shawn continued to perform as a solo artist while working full time as a hospital attendant. It was the kind of cosy arrangement that could well have gone on for years had not Shawn purchased a tape of Daniel O'Donnell from a record stall in Portlaoise. Mightily impressed by Daniel's skill as a vocalist, Shawn decided there and then to turn professional. He secured a loan from the bank, recorded two songs, *Little Nell* and *Dear Old Galway Town*, and sent demos to various companies but to no avail. It was only after he was advised by a friend to contact Shay Hennessy in Smashed Records, now Managing Director of K-tel, that things began to take shape. On hearing Shawn, Shay encouraged him to record three additional songs and release them along with *Little Nell*, a song that was to earn chart success. That was the beginning and, although there have been many difficult times since then, Shawn's singlemindedness has kept him going, and he is now building up an appreciative following in both Ireland and the UK where in 1990 he appeared as special guest on one of Foster & Allen's concert tours.

PROFILE

HOMEPLACE: *Camross, Portlaoise, County Laois*
BIRTHDAY: *May 2*
HEIGHT: *6.00*
COLOUR OF HAIR: *Dark Brown*
COLOUR OF EYES: *Brown*
ABIDING CHILDHOOD MEMORY: *Singing with Big Tom at a dance in the Ossory Club, Borris in Ossory, at the age of seven*
EARLY AMBITIONS: *To be a doctor*
FIRST REAL JOB: *Hospital attendant*
EARLIEST RECORDING AND WHEN: *Blue Hills Of Breffini, 1984*
EARLY MUSICAL INFLUENCES: *Big Tom, Philomena Begley and Margo*
HIGHPOINT IN LIFE TO DATE: *Playing support to Johnny Cash in Castlebar, during his 1988 Irish tour*
UNFULFILLED AMBITION: *To have an international hit record*
FAVOURITE IRISH ARTISTS: *Big Tom, Margo*
FAVOURITE INTERNATIONAL CELEBRITIES: *Loretta Lynn, Kenny Rogers*
FAVOURITE SPORT: *Hurling*
FAVOURITE FILMS: *Startrek, the Rambo films*
FAVOURITE SONG OR MUSICAL ITEM: *Be Careful Of Stones That You Throw*
FAVOURITE NON-SHOWBUSINESS PASTIME: *Visiting my relations, watching films*
WHO WOULD YOU MOST LIKE TO MEET: *Loretta Lynn*
THE QUALITY YOU MOST ADMIRE IN OTHERS: *Modesty*

STAR COMMENT

"It's very important to remain unaffected by success. Being a singer or entertainer shouldn't make you any different."

LARRY CUNNINGHAM

Larry Cunningham is part of showband folklore

*T*here are singers and there are music legends. Larry Cunningham belongs to the second category. Born in Granard, County Longford, Larry had already built up a huge following in neighbouring counties before he gained national prominence with the hit song, *A Tribute To Jim Reeves*, in early 1965. The tribute song not only made it into the Irish Top Ten, but also figured in the British charts, a rare occurrence at that time. Consequently, Larry Cunningham and The Mighty Avons became one of the most sought-after musical combinations in Ireland and the UK.

Prior to that breakthrough Larry had played for a time with The Grafton Band, a Cavan-based outfit. Ironically, the reason he left them was because they had become too popular and Larry felt it was interfering with his day job as a carpenter. However, such was his growing reputation that, when the news broke officially that he was no longer involved with The Grafton Band, Larry was approached by members of St Bridget's Ceili Band, who were on the look-out for a lead singer. Larry refused their invitation on a number of occasions but was persuaded, eventually, and so The Mighty Avons was born.

Then, towards the end of 1965, Larry recorded a double A-sided single, *Lovely Leitrim* and *There Goes That Smile Again*. As it happened, *Lovely Leitrim* was the song everyone wanted to hear, reaching number one and spending fifteen weeks in the Irish charts. In fact, such was its popularity that even to this day, more than a quarter of a century later, it is still linked indelibly with Larry Cunningham. But he is no one-hit wonder and has had close to thirty hit songs in the Irish charts alone. Among the other numbers most closely identified with Larry are: *The Emigrant, Pretty Little Girl From Omagh, I Guess I'm Crazy, Don't Let Me Cross Over, Among The Wicklow Hills, Mother The Queen Of My Heart, Slaney Valley, Snowflakes, The Story Of My Life* and *Hello Mr Peters*, a duet with Margo.

In the late Sixties Larry left the Mighty Avons to front a new band called The Country Blue Boys and still continued to attract big crowds. These days, Larry prefers to take things a little easier and, although he still does some touring, he has cut his public appearances to a minimum.

Larry Cunningham is part of showband folklore and it should never be forgotten that he was one of the most influential Country music performers in the history of Irish show business.

PROFILE

HOMEPLACE: Clooneen, Granard, County Longford
BIRTHDAY: February 13
HEIGHT: 5-10
COLOUR OF HAIR: Brown
COLOUR OF EYES: Blue
ABIDING CHILDHOOD MEMORY: A few of us used to listen to the fill-in programmes on Radio Eireann so that we could learn to play a tune properly. As we had no tape recorders at the time we'd each select a line of the tune and then run out the door so that we wouldn't confuse each other.
EARLY AMBITIONS: To be a priest
FIRST REAL JOB: Apprentice carpenter
EARLIEST RECORDING AND WHEN: A Tribute To Jim Reeves, 1964
EARLY MUSICAL INFLUENCES: Jim Reeves
HIGHPOINT IN LIFE TO DATE: When I reached number one in the charts with Lovely Leitrim; and topping the bill in Carnegie Hall, New York was very special
UNFULFILLED AMBITION: I would like to play a leading role in the GAA with the sole purpose of improving the image of the sport especially for the youngsters, the grass roots of the organisation
FAVOURITE IRISH ARTISTS: Shay Hutchinson, Philomena Begley
FAVOURITE INTERNATIONAL CELEBRITIES: Terry Wogan, Randy Travis
FAVOURITE SPORT: Gaelic football
FAVOURITE FILMS: The Quiet Man, Crocodile Dundee
FAVOURITE SONG OR MUSICAL ITEM: He'll Have To Go
FAVOURITE NON-SHOWBUSINESS PASTIME: Fishing
WHO WOULD YOU MOST LIKE TO MEET: Rose Kennedy
THE QUALITY YOU MOST ADMIRE IN OTHERS: Honesty and hard work

STAR COMMENT

"To be successful, you must be yourself, don't pretend to be something you're not. Respect those who support and believe in what you do. After all it takes people like them to make people like me."

T R D A L L A S

First-class live performer in the toughest of all professions

*F*rom quiet beginnings in the little village of Mount Temple, County Westmeath, to national acclaim as an accomplished Country entertainer was the road to success travelled by the much respected TR Dallas.

TR, whose real name is Tom Allen, is a brother of Tony Allen of Foster & Allen fame, and another brother, Jack, was one-time lead vocalist with the Midlands cabaret group, Allendale. Reared on a small country farm, Tom came to appreciate music at a very early age and while still very young joined the local church choir. On leaving school the young Tom Allen became an apprentice mechanic and during that period teamed up with a local group and played support to many of the famous showbands of the Sixties, experiencing first hand the very special atmosphere of "big-time" show business.

The late Sixties saw Tom take over as lead singer of The Fine Avons but two years later his career came to an abrupt halt when he underwent surgery for tonsillitis. That setback kept him off the road for a considerable length of time.

After spending some time as a salesman Tom returned to show business by joining Doc Carroll and The Nightrunners, in the company of such future stars as his own brother Tony and Mick Foster, nowadays better known, of course, as Foster & Allen.

Before the end of the Seventies Tom had fronted two further bands, The Sailors, and then the famous Mainliners, for whom he replaced John Glenn as lead vocalist. Later, after leaving The Mainliners and forming his own band, he had a chart hit with a novelty song, *Who Shot JR?* By the time his follow-up single, *It's Hard To Be Humble* was released, Tom Allen had become TR Dallas, and – even better than that – a household name. TR's substantial list of hits have included *Daddy's Girl, Big Tom Doesn't Play Here Anymore, I'm Gonna Hire A Wino, The Last One To Touch Me* and, more recently, *Twenty-one Acres Of Land.*

Through the years TR Dallas has earned a reputation as a first-class live performer in the toughest of all professions.

PROFILE

HOMEPLACE: Mount Temple, Moate, County Westmeath
BIRTHDAY: October 21
HEIGHT: 5-8
COLOUR OF HAIR: Black
COLOUR OF EYES: Hazel
ABIDING CHILDHOOD MEMORY: Visiting my cousins the Tormeys
in Drumraney, near Athlone
EARLY AMBITIONS: To be a mechanic
FIRST REAL JOB: Apprentice mechanic
EARLIEST RECORDING AND WHEN: The Stranger's Me, 1970
EARLY MUSICAL INFLUENCES: Kieran Kelly Céilí Band and Joe Dolan
and The Drifters
HIGHPOINT IN LIFE TO DATE: Being selected as lead vocalist with The Mainliners
UNFULFILLED AMBITION: To present my own TV show
FAVOURITE IRISH ARTISTS: Philomena Begley, Joe Dolan
FAVOURITE INTERNATIONAL CELEBRITIES: Willie Nelson, Dolly Parton
FAVOURITE SPORT: Hurling
FAVOURITE FILMS: I don't watch films
FAVOURITE SONG OR MUSICAL ITEM: The Marino Waltz
FAVOURITE NON-SHOWBUSINESS PASTIME: Relaxing at home with my family
WHO WOULD YOU MOST LIKE TO MEET: Pope John Paul II
THE QUALITY YOU MOST ADMIRE IN OTHERS: Honesty

STAR COMMENT

"Be nice to everybody."

ROLY DANIELS

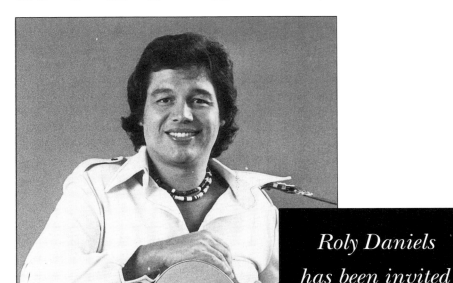

Roly Daniels has been invited to perform in many countries

*T*he mere mention of the name Roly Daniels is enough to jog the memory back to the Sixties. The Seventies, too, were just as spectacularly successful for the man with the magical voice who was born and raised in India.

Music was his first love, and from an early age Roly liked nothing better than entertaining family and friends with a few songs. Even in early childhood he was showing signs of the immense talent and flair that was to take him, eventually, to the very top of show business in his adopted country. Indeed, his interpretation of the old Jimmy Rogers classic, *Mother The Queen of My Heart* – an Irish chart hit for Larry Cunningham – won Roly the top prize in his very first talent contest.

His first interests lay in Country music but, like practically everyone else of that era, he soon caught the Rock and Roll bug. At the age of seventeen Roly was persuaded by Hal Monty, an English comedian, to leave his native India and try his luck in England, where he built up a considerable reputation as a singer who could perform anything from Country to Pop.

Then in the mid-Sixties an invitation to join the Jim Farley band brought Roly to Ireland. Later he joined the Nevada before once again teaming up with Jim Farley to form The Green County Band.

Roly Daniels' first chart hit was *Throw A Little Lovin' My Way* and that was followed over the years by such numbers as *Take A Letter Maria, My Wild Mountain Rose, Don't Forget To Say I Love You, Funny Face* and *The Most Beautiful Girl*. However, the song most closely linked with Roly Daniels is *Hello Darlin,* his powerful version of which reached number two in the Irish charts.

Apart from Britain, Roly Daniels has been invited to perform in many countries, including Canada, France, Sweden, Germany and the US, where he had the honour of representing Ireland at the International Fan Fare in Nashville, Tennessee.

Roly Daniels is a singer of the highest calibre and Ireland can be very proud of her adopted son.

PROFILE

HOMEPLACE: Jabalpur, Central India
BIRTHDAY: May 1
HEIGHT: 6.00½
COLOUR OF HAIR: Black
COLOUR OF EYES: Brown
ABIDING CHILDHOOD MEMORY: Visiting the Taj Mahal in Agra, India and winning a talent competition for singing
EARLY AMBITIONS: To be a Mr Universe and to be a star like Elvis Presley
FIRST REAL JOB: Process Operator in Burmah Shell Oil Refinery in Trombay, Bombay
EARLIEST RECORDING AND WHEN: Bella Bella Marie, 1963
EARLY MUSICAL INFLUENCES: Hank Williams, Eddy Arnold, Elvis Presley and Ray Charles
HIGHPOINT IN LIFE TO DATE: Representing Ireland at the International Fan Fare Festival in Nashville, Tennessee
UNFULFILLED AMBITION: To appear on The Grand Ole Opry Show
FAVOURITE IRISH ARTISTS: Dickie Rock, Sandy Kelly
FAVOURITE INTERNATIONAL CELEBRITIES: Muhammad Ali, Lester Piggott
FAVOURITE SPORT: Horse racing, windsurfing
FAVOURITE FILMS: From Here To Eternity, Song Of Bernadette
FAVOURITE SONG OR MUSICAL ITEM: Green Green Grass Of Home
FAVOURITE NON-SHOWBUSINESS PASTIME: Breeding horses, painting, gardening
WHO WOULD YOU MOST LIKE TO MEET: Mike Tyson
THE QUALITY YOU MOST ADMIRE IN OTHERS: Loyalty

STAR COMMENT

"It's wonderful to be able to trust somebody, but it's even more wonderful for someone to be able to trust you."

THE DIXIES

The Dixies attracted capacity crowds wherever they performed

*M*ore an entertainment outfit than a mere showband, The Dixies are an enormously versatile band from Cork. It was an intense interest in jazz that first brought The Dixies together. Sean Lucey, Joe McCarthy and Theo Cahill, who died many years later while performing on stage, founded the band in the mid-Fifties, calling themselves The Dixielanders.

The fledgling group played support in the Arcadia in Cork to such legendary showbands as The Clipper Carlton, The Royal Showband and the Johnny Quigley Band. Then came the decision to turn professional and shorten their name to the Dixies. Interestingly, that coincided with the signing of a young man called Brendan O'Brien as lead vocalist.

Subsequently, with dance-halls beginning to sprout up all over the country, The Dixies attracted capacity crowds wherever they performed. At the height of their popularity The Dixies were rarely out of the Irish charts, with such songs as: *I'm Counting On You*, their first chart success, *I Love You More Today*, *It's Now Or Never*, *Together Again*, *Save The Last Dance For Me* and *Little Arrows*. Surprisingly, *Little Arrows* was the band's only number one hit, in the Sixties.

Then in 1972 Brendan O'Brien and Joe Mac left The Dixies to front the newly formed Stage 2, and were replaced by Sandy Jones and Joe O'Toole as lead singers. Within a short period Sandy earned the right to represent Ireland in the Eurovision Song Contest, having emerged victorious in the national final with *Ceol an Ghrá*.

In the mid-Seventies, after nearly two decades at the top, The Dixies decided to call it a day. But, by popular demand, the much-loved combination, marked by the return of Brendan O'Brien and Joe Mac, re-formed in 1982, for what was meant to be only a short nostalgic tour. Like all good stories, though, this one had a happy ending and, although Brendan O'Brien is no longer with them, The Dixies, now with Terry McCarthy on lead vocals, are currently doing good business around the country. "The Leeside Legends" still reign supreme.

PROFILE

JOE MCCARTHY

HOMEPLACE: *Copley Street, Cork City*
BIRTHDAY: *August 6*
HEIGHT: *5-10½*
COLOUR OF HAIR: *Fair*
COLOUR OF EYES: *Blue*
ABIDING CHILDHOOD MEMORY: *Getting my first pair of roller skates at the age of eight as a reward for having to wear glasses. I was the butt of all jokes at school and that's probably why I developed a sharp wit.*
EARLY AMBITIONS: *To be an entertainer*
FIRST REAL JOB: *Apprentice upholsterer*
EARLIEST RECORDING AND WHEN: *All Together Now, 1966*
EARLY MUSICAL INFLUENCES: *My mother, Louis Armstrong, Chris Barber*
HIGHPOINT IN LIFE TO DATE: *Being brought out to America by music promoter Bill Fuller*
UNFULFILLED AMBITION: *Don't really have any, just to stay healthy*
FAVOURITE IRISH ARTISTS: *Ray Lynam, Honor Heffernan*
FAVOURITE INTERNATIONAL CELEBRITIES: *Frank Sinatra, Jack Charlton*
FAVOURITE SPORT: *Hurling*
FAVOURITE FILMS: *The Flight Of The Phoenix, Swiss Family Robinson*
FAVOURITE SONG OR MUSICAL ITEM: *Pavarotti singing Pagliacci*
FAVOURITE NON-SHOWBUSINESS PASTIME: *Sailing*
WHO WOULD YOU MOST LIKE TO MEET: *Mother Teresa*
THE QUALITY YOU MOST ADMIRE IN OTHERS: *Sense of humour*

STAR COMMENT

"Enjoy yourself and try to laugh every day. If you have children try and spend time with them and watch them grow. Give them yourself and not just presents."

JOE DOLAN

> *It is as a live performer that Joe Dolan makes his most powerful impact*

Joe Dolan has long been regarded as one of Ireland's most dynamic musical ambassadors. Since the early Sixties the man from Mullingar with a magical voice and indefinable magnetism has thrilled audiences all over the world: in Britain, the US, and as far afield as Australia and the USSR.

Joe's popularity with enthusiasts of diverse musical tastes has earned him legendary status. He first came to prominence when his magnificent version of *The Answer To Everything* made it into the Irish charts. Prior to that Joe had pursued two separate careers, one as a printer in the *Westmeath Examiner* newspaper and the other as a part-time musician in a local group.

In 1964 the recording of *The Answer To Everything* made Joe Dolan and The Drifters household names. To this day that instant hit still remains one of the highlights of Joe's remarkably successful career.

In 1969 his recording of that great standard, *Make Me An Island*, gained him international recognition. The song received powerplay on Radio Luxembourg, ensuring that it was played on the hour every hour. Consequently, as well as making it to number three in the British charts, a remarkable achievement at that time, the song also reached the number one spot in many European countries.

Over the years Joe Dolan has been no stranger to Irish chart success, having made it to number one on numerous occasions with such standards as *House With The Whitewashed Gable*, *Pretty Brown Eyes*, *Teresa*, *I Need You* and *More and More*, which topped the home charts in the early Eighties. He also charted with a string of other hits, including *My Own Peculiar Way*, *Aching Breaking Heart*, *I Love You More Everyday*, *Tar And Cement*, *Sister Mary*, *Wait Till The Clouds Roll By*, *Good Looking Woman*, *It's You It's You*, *It's You* and *Deeper And Deeper*, many of them released on a recent *Greatest Hits* album. But it is as a live performer that Joe Dolan makes his most powerful impact. His ultra-professional shows are always entertaining in the extreme as he performs all his classic hits to audiences of every musical persuasion.

Even today, after a lifetime working on the music scene, Joe Dolan never delivers anything but his best. Truly, there's no show like a "Joe Show". He is a living legend and an international superstar of the very highest calibre.

PROFILE

HOMEPLACE: Mullingar, County Westmeath
BIRTHDAY: October 16
HEIGHT: 5-9
COLOUR OF HAIR: Brown
COLOUR OF EYES: Grey/Green
ABIDING CHILDHOOD MEMORY: Winning the "Beginners Please" competition in the County Hall, Mullingar, because my pal Jazzer Mulligan and all his friends clapped louder for me than anyone else and, since the competition was decided on a clapometer, I won
EARLY AMBITIONS: Not to have to work for a living
FIRST REAL JOB: Apprentice printer
EARLIEST RECORDING AND WHEN: Answer To Everything, 1964
EARLY MUSICAL INFLUENCES: My mother playing the fiddle
HIGHPOINT IN LIFE TO DATE: Our sell-out tour of the USSR in 1981
UNFULFILLED AMBITION: To record a duet with Whitney Houston and then take her out to dinner
FAVOURITE IRISH ARTISTS: The Fureys, Nita Norry
FAVOURITE INTERNATIONAL CELEBRITIES: Dennis Taylor, Christy O'Connor Jr
FAVOURITE SPORT: Golf
FAVOURITE FILMS: All horror films, Shane
FAVOURITE SONG OR MUSICAL ITEM: Nessun Dorma, The Legend Of The Glass Mountain
FAVOURITE NON-SHOWBUSINESS PASTIME: Playing golf
WHO WOULD YOU MOST LIKE TO MEET: President Gorbachev
THE QUALITY YOU MOST ADMIRE IN OTHERS: Honesty

STAR COMMENT

"I cannot think of any other job that would give me the satisfaction of show business. When I'm on stage I want to reach out to everybody and, together with my audience, we have a great time."

TOMMY DRENNAN

Boolavogue *was an instant chart hit and there followed a stream of hit singles*

*A*lthough well over twenty-five years have elapsed since his powerful version of *Boolavogue* raced into the Irish charts, it remains one of the most popular songs in Tommy Drennan's musical reportoire. As the *Hucklebuck* is to Brendan Bowyer so, too, *Boolavogue* is to Tommy Drennan, a song which will always be linked more closely to him than to any other singer. That same song was mainly responsible for setting Tommy Drennan and his band, The Monarchs, on the high road to stardom.

Ironically, but for a change of direction in his early career, Tommy might never have recorded *Boolavogue,* or any other similar recording for that matter. Instead, there was a time when the Limerick-born singer seemed destined for a career in classical music. Tommy first started singing as a boy soprano on a Radio Eireann programme, *Newcomers To The Microphone.* He was barely eleven at the time. Subsequently he won many first places at events all over Ireland, including the famous Moores Melodies competition.

On finishing school Tommy secured employment in a local travel agency in his home city of Limerick and later continued in the same line of work in Dublin while pursuing his musical education at the Royal Irish Academy of Music. Change was just around the corner though, because

Tommy caught the showband bug. He became lead vocalist with The Freshmen and toured extensively in the UK and America.

After a time the desire to return to home pastures proved too strong and Tommy left The Freshmen to front the Limerick-based outfit, The Monarchs. Less than a year later *Boolavogue* was an instant chart hit and there followed a stream of hit singles, including *Love Is A Beautiful Song, Beautiful Peace, Little Boy Lost* and *Promise And The Dream*, which spent twelve weeks in the Irish charts.

From his earliest memories Tommy Drennan never wanted to be anything other than a singer. That his boyhood dream should have come true is something for which Tommy is eternally grateful.

PROFILE

HOMEPLACE: *Janesboro, Limerick City*
BIRTHDAY: *October 12*
HEIGHT: *5-11*
COLOUR OF HAIR: *Black*
COLOUR OF EYES: *Green*
ABIDING CHILDHOOD MEMORY: *Playing makeshift cricket with a hurley stick. We called it Kit Kat. I also remember the hot summers, sunshine and the heat of the pavements.*
EARLY AMBITIONS: *To be a singer*
FIRST REAL JOB: *A clerk in Shannon Travel Agency in Cecil St, Limerick*
EARLIEST RECORDING AND WHEN: *Boolavogue, 1964*
EARLY MUSICAL INFLUENCES: *Nelson Eddy and Pat Boone*
HIGHPOINT IN LIFE TO DATE: *Reaching the number one spot with O Holy Night at Christmas 1982*
UNFULFILLED AMBITION: *To have an international hit*
FAVOURITE IRISH ARTISTS: *Ray Lynam, Twink*
FAVOURITE INTERNATIONAL CELEBRITIES: *Glen Campbell, Pavarotti*
FAVOURITE SPORT: *Squash*
FAVOURITE FILMS: *Lawrence Of Arabia, The Longest Day*
FAVOURITE SONG OR MUSICAL ITEM: *Beethoven's Fifth Symphony*
FAVOURITE NON-SHOWBUSINESS PASTIME: *Walking*
WHO WOULD YOU MOST LIKE TO MEET: *Mother Teresa*
THE QUALITY YOU MOST ADMIRE IN OTHERS: *Kindness*

STAR COMMENT

"I would like to see people becoming more tolerant of each other's views."

DUBLIN CITY RAMBLERS

One of the most popular folk and ballad groups on the Irish music scene

*E*ven though only two of its original members feature in the present line-up, the Dublin City Ramblers remain as one of the most popular folk and ballad groups on the Irish music scene today.

The group was formed in the early Sixties by Patsy Watchorn, inspired as he was by such legends as The Dubliners and The Clancys. Now, over a quarter of a century and several gold discs later, the Dublin City Ramblers are almost as well known and popular in the US as they are in their native city; no surprise when one considers that many of the youngsters who supported the ballad boom in Ireland in the early Eighties have been forced by circumstance to emigrate to America and other farflung destinations. Consequently the Dublin City Ramblers spend much of their time abroad and undertake a twice-yearly, month-long tour of the States. During one of their US sojourns lead vocalist Patsy Watchorn was delighted to be given the opportunity to make a presentation to one of his all-time favourite film stars, Maureen O'Hara. Patsy met Maureen while he was performing at a gala fund-raising concert held in New York in honour of the world-famous Irish actress.

Since their formation The Dublin City Ramblers have rarely been out of the Irish charts, thanks to such favourites as *The Rare Ould Times, The*

Ferryman, Flight Of Earls, The Punch and Judy Man and *Right, Alright*, still one of the most frequently requested songs in their repertoire.

In 1989 Kevin Molloy and Philip McCaffrey, two members of the group, left for pastures new and were replaced by two first-rate musicians, Paul Finlay and Paddy Sweeney, himself a former member of Barleycorn.

The past years have seen The Dublin City Ramblers scale the heights in the music world. Much to the delight of their followers, the "new look" multi-talented group has continued to maintain an exceptionally high standard in their every performance.

PROFILE

PATSY WATCHORN: LEAD VOCALIST

HOMEPLACE: Crumlin, Dublin
BIRTHDAY: October 16
HEIGHT: 5-11
COLOUR OF HAIR: Brown
COLOUR OF EYES: Hazel
ABIDING CHILDHOOD MEMORY: I spent all my holidays at my mother's homeplace in Tunduff near Abbeyleix, County Laois. I couldn't wait to get there, and when my family came to collect me I used to run up the fields and hide. They would pretend to drive away and when I'd come back to the house they'd catch me.
EARLY AMBITIONS: To be another Elvis Presley
FIRST REAL JOB: Working as a despatch clerk in Brownlee Brothers
EARLIEST RECORDING AND WHEN: Three Lovely Lassies From Kimmage, 1964
EARLY MUSICAL INFLUENCES: Eddie Cochrane, John McCormack
HIGHPOINT IN LIFE TO DATE: Being given the keys of Fort Lauderdale and Hollywood, both in Florida
UNFULFILLED AMBITION: To have a number one hit in the Irish charts
FAVOURITE IRISH ARTISTS: The Fureys, Anne Byrne
FAVOURITE INTERNATIONAL CELEBRITIES: Maureen O'Hara and Muhammad Ali
FAVOURITE SPORT: Boxing
FAVOURITE FILMS: The Quiet Man, The Magnificent Seven
FAVOURITE SONG OR MUSICAL ITEM: Don't Cry For Me Argentina
FAVOURITE NON-SHOWBUSINESS PASTIME: Watching sport on television
WHO WOULD YOU MOST LIKE TO MEET: Frank Sinatra
THE QUALITY YOU MOST ADMIRE IN OTHERS: Loyalty

STAR COMMENT

"Be good to others, especially those who are suffering or in need."

THE DUBLINERS

It was Luke Kelly who suggested they call themselves The Dubliners

*I*t all began for the Dubliners in O'Donoghue's Pub in Merrion Row almost thirty years ago. At first they were known as the Ronnie Drew Group and it was the late lamented Luke Kelly who suggested they call themselves The Dubliners.

The newly named group soon emerged as a formidable force on the Irish folk scene. A breakthrough occurred in 1963 when The Dubliners' brand of music created quite a stir at the Edinburgh Festival, and as a result the group became an important part of the "new wave" of the Irish and British folk scene. Consequently The Dubliners found themselves much in demand at folk clubs, concert halls and festivals as well as on numerous television shows, both at home and abroad.

In 1966 their song, *Nelson's Farewell*, brought The Dubliners their first recording success when it reached number six in the Irish charts. Less than a year later the group had a major hit with *Seven Drunken Nights*, a song which reached not only the number one spot in the Irish charts but also number five in the British charts, resulting in a memorable and historic appearance on the BBC *Top of the Pops* programme. This took the group from the folk world into the mainstream of popular music and at the same time brought Irish music to the forefront on the international scene.

Twenty years after that initial appearance The Dubliners featured a second time in the British charts, when they collaborated with The Pogues and reached number eight with a rousing version of *The Irish Rover*. Among the other chart songs closely identified with the Dubliners are: *All For Me Grog, Never Wed An Old Man, Dirty Old Town, Hand Me Down My Bible* and *Free The People*.

Over the years The Dubliners have been a headline act at most of the major concert halls all over Europe. Add to that numerous trips to Australia, New Zealand, Canada, the US and even Iceland, and you begin to realise just how popular the Dubliners really are. Today, The Dubliners are as busy as ever, bringing the spirit of Ireland's capital city to audiences of millions all over the world.

PROFILE

RONNIE DREW

HOMEPLACE: *Dun Laoghaire, County Dublin*
BIRTHDAY: *September 16*
HEIGHT: *5-8*
COLOUR OF HAIR: *Grey*
COLOUR OF EYES: *Blue*
ABIDING CHILDHOOD MEMORY: *Going to Leopardstown Racecourse with my brothers. I always loved the horses and it's an interest I still have.*
EARLY AMBITIONS: *I never really had any ambitions, I just drifted into show business*
FIRST REAL JOB: *Apprentice electrician*
EARLIEST RECORDING AND WHEN: *The Dubliners Album, 1964*
EARLY MUSICAL INFLUENCES: *Listening to Radio Eireann programmes like Ballad Makers Saturday Night and Ceolta Tire. Later Seán Mac Dhonnacha was a great influence.*
HIGHPOINT IN LIFE TO DATE: *The Late Late Special on The Dubliners*
UNFULFILLED AMBITION: *To win the lottery*
FAVOURITE IRISH ARTISTS: *Niall Toibin, Margaret Barry*
FAVOURITE INTERNATIONAL CELEBRITIES: *Luciano Pavarotti, Paul Scofield*
FAVOURITE SPORT: *Horse racing*
FAVOURITE FILMS: *A Man For All Seasons, Ruling Class*
FAVOURITE SONG OR MUSICAL ITEM: *Depends on the mood I'm in*
FAVOURITE NON-SHOWBUSINESS PASTIME: *Walking in the mountains*
WHO WOULD YOU MOST LIKE TO MEET: *No one in particular although I would like to meet the man who hands out the lottery tickets*
THE QUALITY YOU MOST ADMIRE IN OTHERS: *Naturalness*

STAR COMMENT

"If I had my life to live over again, I'd certainly choose another career."

MARY DUFF

> *Mary has appeared on many major international shows*

Acknowledged as one of Ireland's foremost female entertainers, Mary Duff would like to be regarded as a singer of good songs rather than be labelled as a particular kind of singer. Her greatest success to date, though, was winning the 1989 European Gold Star Award, the Country music equivalent of the Eurovision Song Contest. That triumph, in the small Dutch town of Beekse, Bergen, made Mary into a headline star, much in demand for festival appearances in Belgium, Holland, Switzerland and the UK.

Mary, winner of the 1990/91 Most Popular British Female Vocalist award and the 1990 Country N' Irish *RTE Guide* Favourite Female Vocalist award, first appeared in public at the tender age of twelve when she accompanied her accordion-playing father, Tom, at local events. After leaving school she joined a semi-professional group and adeptly combined her singing activities with daytime secretarial work in a local school.

The experience gleaned from her childhood performances ensured that Mary wasn't lacking in confidence when she joined the popular chart group, Jukebox. All the while, however, Mary was determined to make it as a solo performer and she continued to appear in various talent contests. At one such competition she was spotted by Seán Reilly, manager of Daniel

O'Donnell, and immediately he signed her to a management contract. A Ritz recording deal followed, and suddenly Mary Duff was striding purposefully towards stardom. Concert appearances with Daniel O'Donnell are a regular feature of her itinerary and Mary has also appeared on many major international shows, including the prestigious International Country Music Festival at Wembley.

The music business is tough and uncomprising and Mary Duff deserves great credit for attaining such tremendous success so early in her career.

PROFILE

HOMEPLACE: Lobinstown, County Meath
BIRTHDAY: March 6
HEIGHT: 5-4
COLOUR OF HAIR: Brown
COLOUR OF EYES: Blue
ABIDING CHILDHOOD MEMORY: Going to Croke Park with my father
(an All-Ireland medal winner) to watch Meath play
EARLY AMBITIONS: To be a singer
FIRST REAL JOB: School Secretary at Nobber Vocational School, County Meath
EARLIEST RECORDING AND WHEN: Let's Dance, 1982
EARLY MUSICAL INFLUENCES: Patsy Cline
HIGHPOINT IN LIFE TO DATE: Winning the European Gold Star Award in
Holland in 1989
UNFULFILLED AMBITION: To have a number one hit in the Irish and British charts
FAVOURITE IRISH ARTISTS: Daniel O'Donnell, Dolores Keane
FAVOURITE INTERNATIONAL CELEBRITIES: Whitney Houston, Tina Turner
FAVOURITE SPORT: Gaelic football
FAVOURITE FILMS: My Left Foot, Calamity Jane
FAVOURITE SONG OR MUSICAL ITEM: Power Of Love
FAVOURITE NON-SHOWBUSINESS PASTIME: Going for long walks
in the countryside
WHO WOULD YOU MOST LIKE TO MEET: Ricky Skaggs
THE QUALITY YOU MOST ADMIRE IN OTHERS: Genuine sincerity

STAR COMMENT

"You only live once so always do what you're happiest doing."

HUGO DUNCAN

> *Hugo Duncan has never strayed from his Country and Irish roots*

Affectionately known as "The Wee Man From Strabane", Hugo Duncan has been singing his Country and Irish songs for well over twenty years. In the early days Hugo developed a keen interest in music from listening to his mother singing about the house. His musical journey began in earnest when he joined up with some friends to play a weekly date at a local teenage hop. Before that Hugo had won numerous prizes at Feis competitions and had also taken part in various musicals and pantomimes.

Such was his ability as a performer that Hugo secured a position as lead vocalist with The Rhythm Aces while still at school. Later he joined The Arranville Ceili Band as drummer, then moved on to take up the position of singer-guitarist with The Dermot Dunne Céilí Band before teaming up as lead vocalist with The Comets.

Subsequently Hugo Duncan performed as a solo artist on the local pub circuit until he was offered a prominent position with the famed Melody Aces line-up. All the while, however, he continued to enter talent contests, and at one such competition he was approached by Pio McCann to join his band, The Polka Dots.

Some time later Hugo entered the Reach For A Star talent competition on RTE television and finished a creditable second behind Fran O'Toole. Despite this, nothing could have prepared Hugo for what was about to happen. His recording of *Dear God*, a song he had been featuring regularly in his musical repertoire, proved a big success and remained in the charts for seventeen weeks. Further recording successes followed with numbers such as: *Three-Leafed Shamrock*, *Eileen O'Grady*, *Cry Cry Again*, *The Old Bog Road* and *Two Of The Usual*, earning lengthy stays in the Irish charts.

Hugo Duncan has never strayed from his Country and Irish roots and that, allied to his intelligent choice of material, ensures that his popularity is as great today as it ever was.

PROFILE

HOMEPLACE: *Townsend Street, Strabane, County Tyrone*
BIRTHDAY: *March 26*
HEIGHT: *5-6*
COLOUR OF HAIR: *Light Brown*
COLOUR OF EYES: *Green*
ABIDING CHILDHOOD MEMORY: *Growing up in Townsend Street and singing at all the "Guest Teas" in Saint Patrick's Hall*
EARLY AMBITIONS: *To be a drummer*
FIRST REAL JOB: *Working in a nylon factory*
EARLIEST RECORDING AND WHEN: *Little Sweetheart, 1971*
EARLY MUSICAL INFLUENCES: *Joe Dolan*
HIGHPOINT IN LIFE TO DATE: *Receiving a gold disc award which was presented in Saint Patrick's Hall in Strabane. It was great to get the award but even more important that the presentation was made in my home town with all my neighbours and friends there to support me.*
UNFULFILLED AMBITION: *To represent Ireland in the Eurovision Song Contest*
FAVOURITE IRISH ARTISTS: *Brian Coll, Philomena Begley*
FAVOURITE INTERNATIONAL CELEBRITIES: *Charles Bronson, Tom T Hall*
FAVOURITE SPORT: *I like all sports*
FAVOURITE FILMS: *Going My Way, The Quiet Man*
FAVOURITE SONG OR MUSICAL ITEM: *Old Dogs And Children And Water Melon Wine*
FAVOURITE NON-SHOWBUSINESS PASTIME: *Watching television and listening to music*
WHO WOULD YOU MOST LIKE TO MEET: *Mother Teresa*
THE QUALITY YOU MOST ADMIRE IN OTHERS: *Honesty*

STAR COMMENT

"In show business watch out for the pitfalls and avoid alcohol if at all possible. A career in music is very rewarding if you treat it properly."

SEÁN DUNPHY

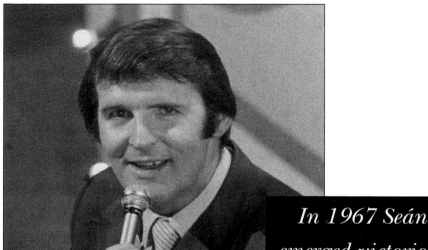

In 1967 Seán emerged victorious in the National Song Contest with **If I Could Choose**

Seán Dunphy is part of Irish showband history. During the Sixties Seán and his band, The Hoedowners, attracted capacity crowds to major dance-halls in Ireland and England, and it was not uncommon for patrons to be turned away, such was the demand to see the band.

Seán's earliest musical influences came from his grandfather, John Farrell, and it was he who enticed young Seán to such places as Dublin's Theatre Royal and Capitol Theatre. Although he was reluctant to go in the beginning, Seán soon developed an intense interest and listened in awe to Martin Crosbie, Seán Mooney and Johnny Keyes. After that he was determined to make a career in show business.

When he left school at the age of fourteen Seán became an apprentice carpenter and just two years later formed a quartet called The Four Lyrics. Seán and the newly formed group performed at all the usual variety shows and even appeared as guests in the Theatre Royal. In addition, he featured on Radio Eireann programmes such as *Beginners Please* with Roy Croft, *Music In The Air* and *Let's Have Music*.

At the age of seventeen Seán Dunphy took the emigrant boat to England and it was while there that he met his future wife, Lily, who introduced him to Bernard Daly, then manager of the Hibernian Club, Fulham Broadway.

Seán successfully auditioned for the vacant position of resident singer in the club and over the next seven years he combined his singing activities with steady daytime employment as a carpenter. It was during his stint at the Hibernian Club that Seán got his first taste of the showband scene, playing support to such famed outfits as The Clipper Carlton, The Melody Aces and The Capitol.

His reputation as a singer soon spread and Seán returned to Ireland after he received an invitation from Earl Gill to join his band in 1962. Three years later they were offered a television series, *Hoedown Ireland,* and consequently became household names. Then in 1967 Seán emerged victorious in the National Song Contest with *If I Could Choose,* and represented Ireland in the Eurovision Song Contest, where he finished a creditable second behind Sandy Shaw. Later sell-out coast to coast concert tours of America became an important part of the Hoedowners' itinerary.

Today Seán Dunphy mostly performs on the cabaret circuit, and his singing style is still appealing in the changing world of Country music.

PROFILE

HOMEPLACE: *Whitehall, Dublin*
BIRTHDAY: *November 30*
HEIGHT: *6-2*
COLOUR OF HAIR: *Brown turning grey*
COLOUR OF EYES: *Brown*
ABIDING CHILDHOOD MEMORY: *Walking with my grandfather through the fields in Donaghmore, County Meath. He had a great love of nature and taught me so many things.*
EARLY AMBITIONS: *To get involved in show business*
FIRST REAL JOB: *Apprentice carpenter*
EARLIEST RECORDING AND WHEN: *Oh How I Miss You Tonight, 1964*
EARLY MUSICAL INFLUENCES: *The Four Aces, The Ames Brothers and all close harmony groups*
HIGHPOINT IN LIFE TO DATE: *Finishing second with If I Could Choose at the Eurovision Song Contest in Vienna in 1967*
UNFULFILLED AMBITION: *To top the bill in Carnegie Hall, New York*
FAVOURITE IRISH ARTISTS: *Val Doonican, Patricia Cahill*
FAVOURITE INTERNATIONAL CELEBRITIES: *Richard Harris, James Galway*
FAVOURITE SPORT: *Golf*
FAVOURITE FILMS: *The Quiet Man, The Magnificent Seven*
FAVOURITE SONG OR MUSICAL ITEM: *Pal Of My Cradle Days*
FAVOURITE NON-SHOWBUSINESS PASTIME: *Reading, landscape painting*
WHO WOULD YOU MOST LIKE TO MEET: *Richard Harris*
THE QUALITY YOU MOST ADMIRE IN OTHERS: *Honesty*

STAR COMMENT

"They'll carry me out singing."

KATHY DURKAN

Kathy has an intense interest in sport

Music has always played an important role in Kathy Durkan's life. She is a
native of Butlersbridge in the Breffni
county of Cavan. Her father, Eugene
Leddy, was a famous dance-band leader
in the Fifties, and Kathy got to know many of the key music personalities of
the time. She herself enjoyed a rich musical upbringing and became a
proficient accordionist while still very young.

Despite her musical background Kathy, although always maintaining an
interest in singing, waited longer than most before adopting a more
professional approach to her career. She married Andy Durkan in the late
Seventies and the following years were spent making a home for Andy and
their two children, Andreas and Alan. Her eldest son, Andreas, was very ill
as a child, and Kathy spent long periods in a Dublin hospital tending to his
every need. Thankfully, Andreas is now back to full health. During those
trying years Kathy made a vow that if her son ever recovered she would
make a career in show business. Then in the early Eighties Kathy joined
local Cavan group, Cottage, and performed successfully on the pub and
cabaret circuit.

It was while appearing on the RTE television programme *Out And About*
that she achieved her first major break in the business. On the strength of

her television performance she secured a recording contract with Harmac and her recording of *Midnight To Moonlight* launched her on the national music scene. It was voted second most popular song of 1988 by the readers of the *RTE Guide*, and her follow-up album, *Moonlight Reflections*, containing a fine selection of well-known standards, was one of the best-selling albums of that year. Then in 1991 Kathy, acknowledged as a first-rate stage performer, recorded the Rita McNeill composition, *Working Man*, which deservedly earned a Top Five chart placing. Firmly established on the Irish music scene, Kathy now aspires to the challenge of proving she can become the top attraction in the most precarious of all professions.

Aside from music, Kathy has an intense interest in sport. What many of her fans may not know is that she was an excellent footballer and played a starring midfield role on the Cavan ladies' team which won All-Ireland honours in 1977.

Kathy Durkan, clearly enjoying her spell in the limelight, fully deserves the success she has earned so admirably.

PROFILE

HOMEPLACE: *Butlersbridge, County Cavan*
BIRTHDAY: *April 1*
HEIGHT: *5-6*
COLOUR OF HAIR: *Light Brown*
COLOUR OF EYES: *Green*
ABIDING CHILDHOOD MEMORY: *The members of my father's band arriving at our house, most of them on bicycles, and bringing me my favourite sweets, Lucky Numbers*
EARLY AMBITIONS: *To be a singer*
FIRST REAL JOB: *Insurance clerk with New Ireland Assurance*
EARLIEST RECORDING AND WHEN: *Memories album, 1987*
EARLY MUSICAL INFLUENCES: *Joe Dolan*
HIGHPOINT IN LIFE TO DATE: *Appearing at the Wembley International Country Music Festival in 1990*
UNFULFILLED AMBITION: *To have a number one hit*
FAVOURITE IRISH ARTISTS: *Joe Dolan, Mary Black*
FAVOURITE INTERNATIONAL CELEBRITIES: *Steffi Graf, Dolly Parton*
FAVOURITE SPORT: *Gaelic football, soccer, golf*
FAVOURITE FILMS: *The Great Escape, My Left Foot*
FAVOURITE SONG OR MUSICAL ITEM: *If I Could Choose*
FAVOURITE NON-SHOWBUSINESS PASTIME: *Playing golf*
WHO WOULD YOU MOST LIKE TO MEET: *Tom Selleck*
THE QUALITY YOU MOST ADMIRE IN OTHERS: *Good humour*

STAR COMMENT

"Keep both feet on the ground."

MICK FLAVIN

Success hasn't changed him one iota

Mick Flavin is blessed with one of the most distinctive Country voices in the Irish music business.

Although a carpenter by profession, he served an invaluable musical apprenticeship, like many other successful entertainers, working on the local pub and cabaret scene. Incredible as it may seem considering the status he currently enjoys, Mick spent close to thirteen years performing on a part-time basis only before securing the all-important breakthrough. That it took so long before his talent was recognised must rate as one of the great mysteries of Irish Country music.

Encouraged by his close friend, Country singer Declan Nerney, Mick reluctantly decided to record a ten-track cassette. It was an excellent recording and, although he was unaware of it at the time, it proved to be the turning point in his career. Subsequently Mick sent the tape to music promoter, Peter Smith, who was so impressed with Mick's wide-ranging skill as a vocalist that he immediately offered him a contract.

Following a gold disc award for sales of his debut album, *I'm Gonna Make It After All*, the singer, known as "Gentleman Mick", was well on his way to stardom. Since then he has established himself as a first-class live performer, playing to large audiences in Ireland and also in the UK, where he is especially popular. As well as appearing on many major television shows, Mick has guested at numerous prestigious Country music festivals, including Wembley. Furthermore, Mick and his band released an excellent video which was recorded in Whitehall Theatre, Dundee, and contained many of his most popularly requested favourites.

Anyone who knows Mick Flavin will confirm that success hasn't changed him one iota. Rightly acknowledged as one of our foremost Country singers, Mick, who in 1991 recorded a duet album with the "Queen Of Country", Philomena Begley, is still the same down-to-earth man who once earned his living as a carpenter with Longford County Council.

PROFILE

HOMEPLACE: *Gaigue, Ballinamuck, County Longford*
BIRTHDAY: *August 3*
HEIGHT: *6-4*
COLOUR OF HAIR: *Brown*
COLOUR OF EYES: *Brown*
ABIDING CHILDHOOD MEMORY: *Singing Country songs while bringing buckets of water from the well*
EARLY AMBITIONS: *To be a professional singer*
FIRST REAL JOB: *Apprentice carpenter*
EARLIEST RECORDING AND WHEN: *I'm Gonna Make It After All album 1987*
EARLY MUSICAL INFLUENCES: *Hank Williams, Tex Ritter, Jim Reeves*
HIGHPOINT IN LIFE TO DATE: *Quitting the booze*
UNFULFILLED AMBITION: *To travel the world*
FAVOURITE IRISH ARTISTS: *Brian Coll, Philomena Begley*
FAVOURITE INTERNATIONAL CELEBRITIES: *George Jones, Dolly Parton*
FAVOURITE SPORT: *Gaelic football, hurling*
FAVOURITE FILMS: *King of Kings, The Magnificent Seven*
FAVOURITE SONG OR MUSICAL ITEM: *Only Sixteen*
FAVOURITE NON-SHOWBUSINESS PASTIME: *Gardening, fowling*
WHO WOULD YOU MOST LIKE TO MEET: *George Jones*
THE QUALITY YOU MOST ADMIRE IN OTHERS: *Loyalty*

STAR COMMENT

"I hope all the people out there 'Keep Travellin To Flavin.' "

FOSTER & ALLEN

Foster & Allen's albums sell in hundreds of thousands

When Mick Foster approached Tony Allen with a view to forming a musical partnership neither man, no matter how optimistic, could ever have envisaged the success story that was to follow. Now some fifteen years later Foster & Allen are acknowledged internationally as two of Ireland's foremost musical ambassadors, as well known and popular in Melbourne as in Mullingar!

Beginning in 1976 Foster & Allen have recorded a stream of hit singles, many of them deservedly earning long stays in the Irish charts: *Old Flames, I Will Love You All My Life, Sweethearts In The Spring, The Black Sheep, The Blacksmith, Maggie* and *Bunch Of Thyme*. Significantly, *Bunch Of Thyme*, with Tony Allen on vocals, became a Top Twenty hit in the British charts, which meant an appearance on the prestigious BBC *Top Of The Pops* television programme. Furthermore, his superb version of *Maggie* raced to number one in Australia in the early Eighties. Concert appearances in the US, Canada, Australia and England continue to be a sell-out for the popular County Westmeath duo.

Unfortunately for Irish patrons, Foster & Allen will not be performing together on the Irish circuit for the foreseeable future. By mutual consent these long-term friends have agreed that Tony, when not touring overseas with Foster & Allen, should front his own Country band, The Tony Allen Band, mainly on the Irish circuit. Mick Foster, meanwhile, as well as tending his beloved horses, plans to do occasional recording and television work.

From Mount-Temple, near Moate in County Westmeath, Tony Allen comes from a musical background and, encouraged by his parents, Pat and Rose, learned to appreciate music at a very early age. His father played the fiddle and Tony also remembers his mother, who sadly died in 1977, 'as a beautiful singer'. With schooldays behind him Tony played with a succession of bands, among them The Marylanders, Kieran Kelly's Band, The Fine Avons and Doc Carroll and The Nightrunners.

Mick Foster was born in Ballymore-Eustace, County Kildare, but his family moved to Mullingar when Mick was barely twelve years of age. A natural musician, Mick started off with the button accordion and soon progressed to playing the piano accordion. Indeed, he became so proficient that he won the All-Ireland Junior Piano Accordion Championship at the age of sixteen in 1964 and captured the senior title four years later. Mick teamed up with a local band in the mid-Sixties and was later joined by Tony Allen. However, when Tony left to join the Fine Avons, Mick took up a solo residency in Larry's Lounge in Mullingar. This association lasted over seven years. Then in 1975 Mick and Tony found themselves playing together again in The Nightrunners line-up. Not long afterwards Mick and Tony played their first date as Foster & Allen.

Foster & Allen's albums sell, not in hundreds, not even in thousands, but in hundreds of thousands. In fact, they have now progressed from having hit singles to a point where each one of their albums, within a week or so of its release, automatically becomes a Top Twenty hit in the British album charts. In addition, Foster & Allen are now among the Golden Video Sellers, which means that each video release has sold in excess of fifty thousand copies.

Since 1982 Foster & Allen have never been out of the Top 200 in the British album charts and on occasions have had as many as three albums in the Top Fifty. A remarkable achievement by any standards, and testimony to their universal appeal to record buyers of all ages. With each new release outselling the last, the spectacular success of this widely acclaimed partnership seems certain to continue.

PROFILE

MICK FOSTER

HOMEPLACE: *Ballymore Eustace, County Kildare*
BIRTHDAY: *December 6*
HEIGHT: *5-7*
COLOUR OF HAIR: *Grey*
COLOUR OF EYES: *Light Blue*
ABIDING CHILDHOOD MEMORY: *Playing old 78 records on my grandmother's temperamental gramophone*
EARLY AMBITIONS: *To be an accordion player*
FIRST REAL JOB: *Shop assistant*
EARLIEST RECORDING AND WHEN: *Traditional Irish music album, 1972*
EARLY MUSICAL INFLUENCES: *The Clancy Brothers and Tommy Makem, Scotland's Jimmy Shand and Will Starr*
HIGHPOINT IN LIFE TO DATE: *Playing with Jimmy Shand on a recent Foster & Allen video*
UNFULFILLED AMBITION: *To own a Grand National winner*
FAVOURITE IRISH ARTISTS: *Tommy Makem, Philomena Begley*
FAVOURITE INTERNATIONAL CELEBRITIES: *Jon Jo O'Neill, Clint Eastwood*
FAVOURITE SPORT: *National Hunt Racing*
FAVOURITE FILMS: *The "Carry On" films . . . and there were dozens of them*
FAVOURITE SONG OR MUSICAL ITEM: *The Bluebell Polka*
FAVOURITE NON-SHOWBUSINESS PASTIME: *Hunting during the winter*
WHO WOULD YOU MOST LIKE TO MEET: *Muhammad Ali*
THE QUALITY YOU MOST ADMIRE IN OTHERS: *Being unaffected by success*

STAR COMMENT

"Live and let live."

PROFILE

TONY ALLEN

HOMEPLACE: Mount Temple, County Westmeath
BIRTHDAY: February 24
HEIGHT: 5-8
COLOUR OF HAIR: Dark Brown
COLOUR OF EYES: Blue
ABIDING CHILDHOOD MEMORY: Being asked up on stage to play the accordion
at a local dance in the old school in Mount Temple, at the age of fourteen
EARLY AMBITIONS: To be involved in the entertainment business
FIRST REAL JOB: Hardware assistant
EARLIEST RECORDING AND WHEN: Liberation At Large, 1976
EARLY MUSICAL INFLUENCES: The Clancy Brothers & Tommy Makem
HIGHPOINT IN LIFE TO DATE: The discovery that as Foster & Allen we had the
ability to make a living out of the music business
UNFULFILLED AMBITION: None
FAVOURITE IRISH ARTISTS: Joe Dolan, Philomena Begley
FAVOURITE INTERNATIONAL CELEBRITIES: Willie Nelson, Dolly Parton
FAVOURITE SPORT: Snooker and boxing
FAVOURITE FILMS: Any of the Marx Brothers films: Duck Soup, A Night At The
Opera, Monkey Business
FAVOURITE SONG OR MUSICAL ITEM: The Four Star Quartet
playing traditional music
FAVOURITE NON-SHOWBUSINESS PASTIME: Relaxing at home with my family
WHO WOULD YOU MOST LIKE TO MEET: Willie Nelson
THE QUALITY YOU MOST ADMIRE IN OTHERS: Naturalness

STAR COMMENT

"Don't ever worry about anything but, at the same time, do your best always."

THE FUREY BROTHERS AND DAVEY ARTHUR

More than a folk group, they are an integral part of Irish culture

*I*t would be difficult to visualise the Irish entertainment scene without the musical wizardry, energy, colour and charm of The Furey Brothers and Davey Arthur. Somehow traditional music values appear safe as long as this internationally renowned group is around. The father of the four Furey brothers, Ted, was much more than a famous fiddle player: he was a teacher, collector of songs and, above all else, an inspirational figure. The Fureys not surprisingly enjoyed a richly musical upbringing as their mother, Nora, besides playing banjo and accordion, had a wealth of songs and stories to pass on to her offspring. From a very early age, Finbar was a genius on the uileann pipes, while Eddie had few peers on fiddle and guitar.

In 1966 Eddie and Finbar set off to Scotland to deputise for Joe Heaney. Originally the tour was to last twelve days, but instead the lads stayed three years, so well did their combination of pipes and guitar go down with Scottish audiences. Shortly afterwards they joined the Clancy Brothers for a tour of America, which was the beginning of three memorable years. Back in Ireland in the early Seventies The Fureys met a German promoter, Carsten Linde, at the fleadh in Listowel, County Kerry, and he was so impressed that he immediately booked them for a tour of Germany, during which time they became a major attraction.

Back home in Ireland the other two Fureys, Paul and George, had formed a band with Scottish-born Davey Arthur who had learned his trade from Ted Furey. The band was called The Buskers, and after Paul, George and Davey were involved in a car crash, Finbar and Eddie decided it was time to return home to be with them. It wasn't long before the newly formed Furey Brothers and Davey Arthur made a major impact in Ireland with such hits as *Green Fields Of France* (a number one in 1979), *Leaving Nancy, Lonesome Boatman, The Old Man, Now Is The Hour, Steal Away* and another chart-topper, *When You Were Sweet Sixteen,* one of the songs most closely associated with the group.

The Furey Brothers and Davey Arthur are more than a folk group, they are an integral part of Irish culture and, having played a key role in elevating folk to the status it now occupies today, are musical heroes one and all.

PROFILE

FINBAR FUREY

HOMEPLACE: *Ballyfermot, Dublin*

BIRTHDAY: *September 28*   HEIGHT: *5-11*

COLOUR OF HAIR: *Dark Brown*   COLOUR OF EYES: *Green*

ABIDING CHILDHOOD MEMORY: *My father Ted teaching us all how to play different instruments and to use our imagination to respect good music*

EARLY AMBITIONS: *To be an opera singer*

FIRST REAL JOB: *Working with Dan Dowd and Matt Keenan making reeds for other pipers*

EARLIEST RECORDING AND WHEN: *I Know Where I'm Going album with my brother Eddie, and Paddy Bell from Belfast, 1966*

EARLY MUSICAL INFLUENCES: *My father and mother, also Tommy Moore and Johnny Keenan, two local pipers*

HIGHPOINT IN LIFE TO DATE: *Winning the World title at the uileann pipes in 1964*

UNFULFILLED AMBITION: *To have a number one album in the American charts*

FAVOURITE IRISH ARTISTS: *Jim McCann, Dolores Keane, Mary Black*

FAVOURITE INTERNATIONAL CELEBRITIES: *Dave Stewart, Annie Lennox*

FAVOURITE SPORT: *Golf*

FAVOURITE FILMS: *The Fighting Sullivans, Ryan's Daughter*

FAVOURITE SONG OR MUSICAL ITEM: *The Lonesome Boatman*

FAVOURITE NON-SHOWBUSINESS PASTIME: *Spending time with my family passing on the tradition that I myself learned from my parents*

WHO WOULD YOU MOST LIKE TO MEET: *Jack Nicklaus*

THE QUALITY YOU MOST ADMIRE IN OTHERS: *Honesty*

STAR COMMENT

"Put your life into three parts. Give a third to your family, a third to your business and friends and keep a third for yourself."

BRIDIE GALLAGHER

Her first recording proved an instant hit

*B*ridie Gallagher is truly one of the all-time greats of Irish show business. Through the years Bridie's unique style of singing has been heard all over the world, from the London Palladium to the Sydney Opera House.

Bridie, second youngest in a family of ten, grew up in a happy home environment. Her mother, Bridget, possessing a great flair for singing, instilled in young Bridie a love of all things musical. Even to this day Bridie vividly remembers having to do her party piece at family shows.

She attended Massinas National School near Creeslough and while there was encouraged to sing and, not surprisingly, her teacher often got her to perform for the class, a task Bridie disliked intensely. However, she progressed to the local choir and from there to making appearances at local concerts for the Franciscan Friary.

At the tender age of fifteen, Bridie moved to Belfast to live with her aunt and, after appearing at a few concerts in St Mary's Hall, soon began to be noticed. What many people may not know is that Bridie started her career singing Pop songs. The changeover came about when she featured as the closing act at a show in St Columba's Hall, Derry City and, as all her own songs had been performed during the course of the night, Bridie had no option but to sing Irish ballads like *The Whistling Gypsy*, *The Spinning Wheel* and *A Mother's Love's A Blessing*. The reaction was so positive that within a week Bridie had signed a recording contract with Decca Records, London. Her first recording, *A Mother's Love's A Blessing* and *I'll Remember You Love In My Prayers*, proved an instant hit and marked the beginning of an extraordinarily successful career. Among the other hit songs associated with Bridie Gallagher are: *The Boys From The County Armagh*, *Goodbye Johnny Dear*, *Two Little Orphans* and *The Girl From Donegal*.

The ever popular and enduring Bridie Gallagher continues to sing her songs in that unmistakable voice which first brought her to international stardom all those years ago.

PROFILE

HOMEPLACE: Ards, Creeslough, County Donegal
BIRTHDAY: September 7   *HEIGHT: 5-3*
COLOUR OF HAIR: Fair   *COLOUR OF EYES: Blue/Grey*
ABIDING CHILDHOOD MEMORY: A very happy home where there was always music and singing. We used to put a pair of curtains on the kitchen door, used a kitchen table for our stage and each one of the family present did a party piece, dressing up in whatever we could find. It was special.
EARLY AMBITIONS: To be a singer
FIRST REAL JOB: Working in the local post office
EARLIEST RECORDING AND WHEN: A Mother's Love's A Blessing and I'll Remember You Love In My Prayers, 1956
EARLY MUSICAL INFLUENCES: Doris Day, Judy Garland, Vera Lynn, Bing Crosby, Pat Boone
HIGHPOINT IN LIFE TO DATE: Appearing in both the London Palladium and Sydney Opera House, and in Lusaka, Zambia
UNFULFILLED AMBITION: To present a radio or television show
FAVOURITE IRISH ARTISTS: Joe Dolan, Dickie Rock, Philomena Begley
FAVOURITE INTERNATIONAL CELEBRITIES: Julio Iglesias
FAVOURITE SPORT: I love all kinds of sport and I am especially proud of our Irish soccer team
FAVOURITE FILMS: Snow White and The Seven Dwarfs, My Fair Lady
FAVOURITE SONG OR MUSICAL ITEM: People (Barbara Streisand)
FAVOURITE NON-SHOWBUSINESS PASTIME: Oil painting, cookery
WHO WOULD YOU MOST LIKE TO MEET: Pope John Paul II
THE QUALITY YOU MOST ADMIRE IN OTHERS: Honesty, good manners and patience

STAR COMMENT

"I'm very lucky to have made a successful career, which has given me the opportunity to meet so many nice people and travel to so many places. I'm also thankful to be in such good health after undergoing open-heart surgery."

JOHN GLENN

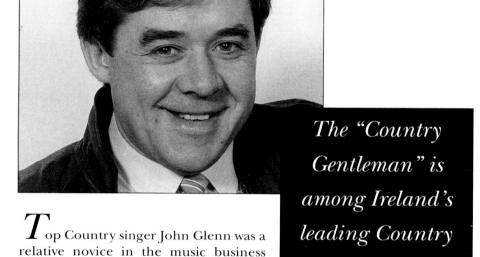

The "Country Gentleman" is among Ireland's leading Country and Irish vocalists

*T*op Country singer John Glenn was a relative novice in the music business when he replaced Big Tom as lead vocalist with The Mainliners. A short time previously Big Tom had left to form his own band, The Travellers and, despite a lack of experience, John was looked upon as an ideal replacement. At the time The Mainliners were one of Ireland's most revered musical combinations, and taking over from Big Tom was an awesome undertaking for the young singer from Crossmaglen, County Armagh.

Within a short time, however, John had established himself as a firm favourite with record buyers and dancers alike. His first recording, *Sunnyside Of The Mountain*, an old Hawkshaw Hawkins number, was an instant chart hit. His superb debut album, also entitled *Sunnyside Of The Mountain*, earned a well-deserved gold disc award.

During the following years John Glenn was a regular in the Irish charts with such hits as *Call Me Darling, Turn Back The Years* and *Little Country Town In Ireland*, which had a lengthy stay in the charts in the late Seventies. John also enjoyed considerable success with the Henry McMahon composition, *The Clones Cyclone*, a tribute song which became hugely popular when Barry McGuigan won the World Featherweight Boxing Title in 1985.

Although he left The Mainliners in 1978 to front his own band, The Wranglers, John has continued to be a big attraction at major venues both here in Ireland and in Britain, where he still enjoys a loyal following. Furthermore, John has a number of American tours to his credit and has appeared at major British festivals, including Roundwood Park and Peterborough.

Since emerging on the music scene in 1975 John Glenn, known as the "Country Gentleman" has become a very popular personality and today is among Ireland's leading Country and Irish vocalists.

PROFILE

HOMEPLACE: *Rathkeelan, Crossmaglen, County Armagh*
BIRTHDAY: *March 22*
HEIGHT: *5-11*
COLOUR OF HAIR: *Brown*
COLOUR OF EYES: *Blue*
ABIDING CHILDHOOD MEMORY: *I remember hearing our near neighbour and family friend, Jamsie Murray, telling my parents many years ago that their fella would one day make his living at the singing. And, you know, Jamsie was right.*
EARLY AMBITIONS: *To be a mechanic*
FIRST REAL JOB: *Apprentice mechanic*
EARLIEST RECORDING AND WHEN: *Sunnyside Of The Mountain, 1975*
EARLY MUSICAL INFLUENCES: *Big Tom*
HIGHPOINT IN LIFE TO DATE: *My very first appearance, after fifteen years in the business, on Ulster Television with Gerry Kelly in April 1990*
UNFULFILLED AMBITION: *To record in Nashville*
FAVOURITE IRISH ARTISTS: *Big Tom, Philomena Begley*
FAVOURITE INTERNATIONAL CELEBRITIES: *Abba, Harvey Smith*
FAVOURITE SPORT: *Gaelic football*
FAVOURITE FILMS: *Dirty Harry, The Quiet Man*
FAVOURITE SONG OR MUSICAL ITEM: *Ramblin' Rose*
FAVOURITE NON-SHOWBUSINESS PASTIME: *Fishing*
WHO WOULD YOU MOST LIKE TO MEET: *Muhammad Ali*
THE QUALITY YOU MOST ADMIRE IN OTHERS: *Honesty*

STAR COMMENT

"I'd like my own children to have a happy and peaceful upbringing, just as I had myself as a boy growing up in Rathkeelan."

G L O R I A

One Day At A Time *spent a staggering ninety weeks in the Irish charts*

*R*egarded as one of Ireland's fore-most vocal stylists, Gloria will forever be identified with her massive hit song, *One Day At A Time*, which spent a staggering ninety weeks in the Irish charts.

From a very early age Gloria Smith began playing piano and accordion under the guidance of her father, himself a proficient musician with The Arcadians. While still attending primary school the talented Gloria appeared on a number of television shows, most notably *Tea Time With Tommy* and *Jamboree*, hosted by Dermot O'Brien. It was a signpost of things to come. Later Gloria studied classical music with Sister de Lourdes.

When Gloria left school she worked as a hotel receptionist while at the same time playing with the family group at weekends. Shortly afterwards she was offered a position as piano player with the Maurice Lynch Show-band and while there she met her future husband, Don Sherry. It was Don who suggested Gloria change her style to Country music. It proved the turning point in her career and she joined the newly formed Cascades as lead vocalist. Her debut promotional single, *Punish Me Tomorrow*, served its purpose and gained her national attention. Later she spent a term with the Johnny McEvoy Band before eventually forming her own group, Mississippi, in collaboration with her husband, Don. Chart success followed with such numbers as *I'll Get Over You, My Younger Days, Pal Of My Cradle Days* and of course *One Day At A Time*. The song, given to Gloria by the composer Marijohn Wilkins, was recorded in Nashville with the sole purpose of including it on an album. Instead it went on to become the record which enjoyed the longest stay ever in Irish chart history.

During the late Seventies, Gloria won practically every music award of note including Top Irish Country Singer and, while she has cut down on her personal appearances in recent years, she retains her star status as one of Ireland's top Country singers.

PROFILE

HOMEPLACE: *Navan, County Meath*
BIRTHDAY: *May 25*
HEIGHT: *5-00*
COLOUR OF HAIR: *Auburn*
COLOUR OF EYES: *Brown*
ABIDING CHILDHOOD MEMORY: *My father taking me on stage to play accordion with him in Kilmoon Ballroom near Ashbourne, County Meath. I was about eight or nine at the time.*
EARLY AMBITIONS: *To be a singer*
FIRST REAL JOB: *Receptionist*
EARLIEST RECORDING AND WHEN: *Punish Me Tomorrow, L.A. International Airport, 1971*
EARLY MUSICAL INFLUENCES: *My father*
HIGHPOINT IN LIFE TO DATE: *One Day At A Time reaching number one in the Irish charts*
UNFULFILLED AMBITION: *To have my own TV series*
FAVOURITE IRISH ARTISTS: *Mary Duff, Roly Daniels*
FAVOURITE INTERNATIONAL CELEBRITIES: *Terry Wogan, Bette Midler*
FAVOURITE SPORT: *Tennis*
FAVOURITE FILMS: *The Rose, Madame X*
FAVOURITE SONG OR MUSICAL ITEM: *Love Story*
FAVOURITE NON-SHOWBUSINESS PASTIME: *Walking with the children*
WHO WOULD YOU MOST LIKE TO MEET: *Pope John Paul II*
THE QUALITY YOU MOST ADMIRE IN OTHERS: *Honesty*

STAR COMMENT

"Treat others as you would like to be treated."

FINBAR HARTE

A name to watch out for on the Irish music scene

Finbar Harte is one of the growing number of newcomers to emerge on the Country and Irish music scene. Barely twenty-one, he possesses the kind of mature sound you'd normally come to expect from a singer twice his age. The County Cavan-born singer first came to national prominence with his powerful rendition of the now popular favourite, *When New York Was Irish*, which became a Top Ten hit even before he had formed his own band.

Finbar's early musical tastes were somewhat different from those of his school friends, who favoured Leo Sayer, Bruce Springsteen, Whitney Houston and George Michael, whereas he liked nothing better than listening to the music of Brian Coll, Frank McCaffrey and Jim Reeves, when growing up near the shores of Lough Sheelin.

With schooldays behind him, Finbar worked in the family pub in Kilnaleck and was often requested to sing a few songs with whatever band would happen to be playing. Encouraged by family and friends, he recorded a four-track cassette which came into the possession of Brian Finlay, a former drummer with The Mighty Avons and now involved in management. It was Brian's idea that Finbar should do a version of a song he had brought back with him from New York. That song was titled, *When New York*

Was Irish, and when the record was launched in the Mansion House, Dublin, by fellow Cavan man, John Wilson, TD (now Tanaiste), and former Dublin Lord Mayor, Sean Haughey, it made an immediate impact. Shortly afterwards in March 1990 *When New York Was Irish*, helped considerably by a major television and radio advertising campaign, entered the Irish charts at number eighteen, before eventually becoming a Top Ten hit.

The next step was the formation of a new five-piece band, the subsequent signing of a recording contract with Dino Entertainment, which was followed by the release of his debut album, *Songs Of Our Land, Songs Of Our Time*.

There is no doubt that his debut album reinforces the feeling that Finbar Harte is a name to watch out for on the Irish music scene.

PROFILE

HOMEPLACE: *Ballyheelan, Kilnaleck, County Cavan*
BIRTHDAY: *July 8*
HEIGHT: *5-7*
COLOUR OF HAIR: *Fair*
COLOUR OF EYES: *Blue*
ABIDING CHILDHOOD MEMORY: *Listening to my father playing the fiddle*
EARLY AMBITIONS: *To become a Country singing star*
FIRST REAL JOB: *Apprentice barman*
EARLIEST RECORDING AND WHEN: *A Mother's Love's A Blessing, 1989*
EARLY MUSICAL INFLUENCES: *Brian Coll, Jim Reeves, Frank McCaffrey*
HIGHPOINT IN LIFE TO DATE: *Playing to a crowd of over two thousand at an open air concert in Kilnaleck*
UNFULFILLED AMBITION: *To have a number one hit*
FAVOURITE IRISH ARTISTS: *Brian Coll, Philomena Begley*
FAVOURITE INTERNATIONAL CELEBRITIES: *Nanci Griffith, Charley Pride*
FAVOURITE SPORT: *Darts*
FAVOURITE FILMS: *Rhinestone, Robo Cop*
FAVOURITE SONG OR MUSICAL ITEM: *From A Distance*
FAVOURITE NON-SHOWBUSINESS PASTIME: *Fishing, listening to music*
WHO WOULD YOU MOST LIKE TO MEET: *Clint Black*
THE QUALITY YOU MOST ADMIRE IN OTHERS: *The ability to entertain and a professional attitude to the music business*

STAR COMMENT

"In a tough business, I hope to be accepted by the Irish people for what I have to contribute."

DERMOT HEGARTY

This year is the twenty-first anniversary of the original release of **Twenty-one Years**

*I*t is said that every cloud has its silver lining. Nobody knows that better than Dermot Hegarty, whose love for music goes back to his earliest years.

It was while recuperating from an accident that Dermot was asked to appear as a solo artist in the Longford Arms Hotel. Mick Clerkin of King Records, now managing director of the highly successful Ritz label, saw him perform and was so impressed by the young Longford-born singer that he added him to his roster of artists. In 1967 Dermot's first record, *Shores Of Amerikay*, reached number four in the Irish charts, and the follow-up single, *Mary Ann Regrets*, was another runaway success.

Before the end of the Sixties Dermot had launched his own band, The Plainsmen, and also formed Release Records in partnership with Mick Clerkin and RTE sports commentator, Jimmy Magee. Dermot's most spectacular success was his recording of *Twenty-one Years*, which became a number one hit and spent a total of thirty-nine weeks in the Irish charts. In fact, this year is the twenty-first anniversary of the original release of *Twenty-one Years*, and as a result Dermot has been the recipient of many awards to mark the happy occasion.

Among Dermot's other chart successes were *Two Little Girls In Blue, Love Is Teasing, Four Green Fields, Only Her Rivers Run Free* and *After Twenty-one Years*, a Top Ten hit in the early Seventies.

With the emergence of a vibrant cabaret scene in Ireland during the early Seventies, Dermot left The Plainsmen to front his own three-piece band. He also toured extensively in the UK, Canada and the US. In recent times the popular singer has made a welcome return to the Irish cabaret and ballroom circuit with a newly formed band, The New Plainsmen.

Dermot Hegarty remains a popular performer on the Irish music scene and his singing is as appealing today as at any other time in his long and successful career.

PROFILE

HOMEPLACE: Longford Town
BIRTHDAY: October 6
HEIGHT: 5-10
COLOUR OF HAIR: Black/Grey
COLOUR OF EYES: Blue
ABIDING CHILDHOOD MEMORY: Walking the cattle to the fair on a winter's morning
EARLY AMBITIONS: To become a priest
FIRST REAL JOB: Assembling televisions at the Philips plant in Clonskeagh, Dublin
EARLIEST RECORDING AND WHEN: The Shores Of Amerikay, 1967
EARLY MUSICAL INFLUENCES: Mario Lanza
HIGHPOINT IN LIFE TO DATE: Topping the bill at Carnegie Hall, New York
UNFULFILLED AMBITION: To discover and promote a new Irish talent
FAVOURITE IRISH ARTISTS: Johnny McEvoy, Louise Morrissey
FAVOURITE INTERNATIONAL CELEBRITIES: Neil Diamond, Rod Steiger
FAVOURITE SPORT: None
FAVOURITE FILMS: Gone With The Wind, The Killing Fields
FAVOURITE SONG OR MUSICAL ITEM: Theme music from Evita
FAVOURITE NON-SHOWBUSINESS PASTIME: Reading and watching television
WHO WOULD YOU MOST LIKE TO MEET: President Gorbachev
THE QUALITY YOU MOST ADMIRE IN OTHERS: Tolerance

STAR COMMENT

"If to your own self you cannot be true, then you cannot be true to anyone."

JOHN HOGAN

> *When he arrived at Slane Studios all John Hogan had with him was a guitar and a song in his heart*

*I*t was always John Hogan's ambition to become a professional entertainer but, like others before him, the genial West-meath man suffered one setback after another, chasing what seemed like an elusive dream. All that changed in 1987.

John took it upon himself to spend his mortgage money to record a song called *Brown Eyes* which his mother had learned as a child. By any standards it was a risky undertaking. When he arrived at Slane Studios on that special day over four years ago, all John Hogan had with him was a guitar in a cardboard box and a song in his heart. There was no need to worry, though, because *Brown Eyes* proved to be a magical recording, earning Top Ten status with sales in excess of ten thousand.

John Hogan's early years were spent working as a supervisor in a local Bord na Móna briquette factory in Croghan, County Offaly, but even at that stage his flair for music was evident and he often entertained his colleagues with a few songs. Shortly after the success of *Brown Eyes*, John decided to give up his steady job to concentrate on a full-time career in show business. The subsequent formation of a new band, plus a prime time slot on RTE television's *Late Late Show*, put John Hogan on course to fulfilling his dream. Indeed, such were the demands in the beginning that

John had to work seven days a week for the first six months. This hard work paid dividends and soon John was attracting large crowds at many of the major venues around the country. Although the whole area of show business was all very new to John – who was more used to the quiet and simple life – he nevertheless enjoyed the excitement immensely.

In late 1990 John signed a major contract with Ritz Records and immediately entered the Irish charts with the Dillon/Overstreet composition, *Still Got A Crush On You.*

Anyone who is acquainted with John knows that success hasn't changed him at all. He still retains that warm friendly demeanour and continues to live in County Offaly close to the briquette factory where he first dreamed the dream that was to become a reality.

PROFILE

HOMEPLACE: *Kilbeggan, County Westmeath*
BIRTHDAY: *August 31*
HEIGHT: *5-8*
COLOUR OF HAIR: *Black*
COLOUR OF EYES: *Blue*
ABIDING CHILDHOOD MEMORY: *Walking with mother to my aunt's house in Rostella, where we'd sit singing songs and telling stories by the light of the fire*
EARLY AMBITIONS: *To be a singer*
FIRST REAL JOB: *Apprentice fitter*
EARLIEST RECORDING AND WHEN: *Brown Eyes, 1987*
EARLY MUSICAL INFLUENCES: *Jim Reeves, Hank Williams*
HIGHPOINT IN LIFE TO DATE: *First appearance on the Late Late Show*
UNFULFILLED AMBITION: *To spend a year in a log cabin on a mountain away from everything*
FAVOURITE IRISH ARTISTS: *Paddy O'Brien, Linda Martin*
FAVOURITE INTERNATIONAL CELEBRITIES: *Buck Owens, George Jones*
FAVOURITE SPORT: *Athletics*
FAVOURITE FILMS: *My Left Foot, Papillon*
FAVOURITE SONG OR MUSICAL ITEM: *Your Cheatin' Heart*
FAVOURITE NON-SHOWBUSINESS PASTIME: *Walking*
WHO WOULD YOU MOST LIKE TO MEET: *Pope John Paul II*
THE QUALITY YOU MOST ADMIRE IN OTHERS: *Sincerity*

STAR COMMENT

"Always have time for other people."

R E D   H U R L E Y

In 1989, he had the honour of singing to a capacity audience which included President Bush

Red Hurley possesses the kind of voice that immediately makes you sit up and take notice. Bearing that in mind, it is not surprising that the popular entertainer has had many offers from abroad, including the opportunity to sign a major contract with RCA Records in 1971. However, Red and his band were doing so well in Ireland at the time that he reluctantly declined the offer.

In 1968, at an early stage in Red Hurley's career, fate dictated a change. Red, a drummer with a Dublin-based band at the time, was involved in a car accident on his way home from a gig. He suffered injuries to his shoulder and ankle which meant that he couldn't play the drums for some months. To Red's surprise, however, the manager of the pub where he used to play invited him to do some singing. Although he was initially reluctant he was persuaded to take that step which was to lead to stardom.

Shortly after the initial breakthrough Red auditioned for and secured the position as lead vocalist with The Colours. His first single, *Poor Man's Roses*, spent four weeks in the Irish charts and helped establish him on the national music scene. Then about six months later Red formed a band called The Wheels, before moving on to team up with The Nevada. Indeed, it was while with The Nevada that Red enjoyed his first number one hit,

Sometimes, in 1971. His follow-up single, *Kiss Me Goodbye,* also made it to the top of the Irish charts. Red has fond memories of his time with The Nevada, one of the major attractions on the Irish music scene, playing six nights a week to capacity audiences. Nowadays, Red Hurley continues to perform at cabaret and dancehall venues and he has also presented his own television series. He spends considerable time touring in America and during a concert in 1989, at a convention in Houston, Texas, he had the honour of singing to a capacity audience which included the President of the United States, George Bush.

Red Hurley freely admits he's having a great time doing what he likes best and looks forward to continuing for many years to come.

PROFILE

HOMEPLACE: *Milltown, Dublin*
BIRTHDAY: *November 11*
HEIGHT: *5-10½*
COLOUR OF HAIR: *Brown*
COLOUR OF EYES: *Blue*
ABIDING CHILDHOOD MEMORY: *Going to the seaside with my Mum and Dad at Merrion Strand*
EARLY AMBITIONS: *To play drums*
FIRST REAL JOB: *Draughtsman*
EARLIEST RECORDING AND WHEN: *Poor Man's Roses, 1969*
EARLY MUSICAL INFLUENCES: *Father and Mother, Motown music*
HIGHPOINT IN LIFE TO DATE: *Having a number one hit and that very same day receiving a telephone call telling me that I had been voted "Singer Of The Year" for 1971*
UNFULFILLED AMBITION: *To have an international hit*
FAVOURITE IRISH ARTISTS: *Joe Dolan, Twink*
FAVOURITE INTERNATIONAL CELEBRITIES: *Jane Fonda, Jack Nicholson*
FAVOURITE SPORT: *Golf*
FAVOURITE FILMS: *The Godfather films*
FAVOURITE SONG OR MUSICAL ITEM: *Phantom Of The Opera*
FAVOURITE NON-SHOWBUSINESS PASTIME: *Playing golf*
WHO WOULD YOU MOST LIKE TO MEET: *Seve Ballesteros*
THE QUALITY YOU MOST ADMIRE IN OTHERS: *Sincerity*

STAR COMMENT

"Life is a take, not a rehearsal."

THE INDIANS

They have one of the most loyal followings in Irish show business

Now over twenty years on the road, that colourful and energetic band, The Indians, have lost none of their popular appeal. Acknowledged as a fine dance-band and noted for their wide-ranging musical repertoire which comprises Country, Pop, Rock and Roll and a selection of their own material, The Indians have never been off the road since they were first formed back in January 1971.

They started out calling themselves The Casino and it was only when they changed their name to The Indians – wearing authentic Red Indian costumes – that the band began to command attention. Almost immediately there was a noticeable increase in attendances at their live performances. In addition, The Indians were awarded a gold disc for sales of their debut album, *Indian Country*. Among the songs featured on the big-selling album were: *Squaws Along The Yukon*, *The Wigwam Wiggle* and *Son Don't Go Near The Indians*.

In the intervening years The Indians have concentrated their efforts more on pleasing their followers with their lively stage performances than on making records. The Indians are hugely popular in Britain and have topped the bill at the famous Roundwood Festival on many occasions. Despite the difficult phase in the mid-Eighties which saw a decline in the live music business, The Indians, unlike many other renowned combinations, continued playing together. That they survived is due in no small way to their professionalism and their intense love of music. Today The Indians, who took over their own management in 1987, continue to feature at many of the major dance-band venues in Ireland and also appear regularly at Country clubs throughout the UK.

Above all else The Indians are a fine dance-band and are extremely pleased that they have one of the most loyal followings in Irish show business.

PROFILE

NOEL BRADY: LEAD VOCALIST

HOMEPLACE: *Cabra West, Dublin City*
BIRTHDAY: *December 28*
HEIGHT: *6-3*
COLOUR OF HAIR: *Brown*
COLOUR OF EYES: *Blue*
ABIDING CHILDHOOD MEMORY: *My first day at school in St Saviour's*
EARLY AMBITIONS: *To be a singer*
FIRST REAL JOB: *Paper boy*
EARLIEST RECORDING AND WHEN: *Wigwam Wiggle, 1971*
EARLY MUSICAL INFLUENCES: *Elvis Presley*
HIGHPOINT IN LIFE TO DATE: *The day I joined the Casino band*
UNFULFILLED AMBITION: *To have met Elvis Presley*
FAVOURITE IRISH ARTISTS: *Sandy Kelly, Brendan Grace*
FAVOURITE INTERNATIONAL CELEBRITIES: *Cliff Richard,*
Jack Charlton
FAVOURITE SPORT: *Soccer*
FAVOURITE FILMS: *Help, G I Blues*
FAVOURITE SONG OR MUSICAL ITEM: *Love Me Tender*
FAVOURITE NON-SHOWBUSINESS PASTIME: *Watching football*
WHO WOULD YOU MOST LIKE TO MEET: *Pope John Paul II*
THE QUALITY YOU MOST ADMIRE IN OTHERS: *Honesty*

STAR COMMENT

"If you appreciate your audience, they'll appreciate you."

GEORGE KANE

George Kane is a happy man, doing what he likes best

Geeorge Kane loves to sing and there is no doubt he has a style all his own. Born in Tullamore, County Offaly, but now living in Tralee, County Kerry, George was introduced to music at a very early age by his father, a sax player with the local Kelly's Dance Band. When the family moved to England his father hired a music teacher who taught a reluctant George piano. Like most youngsters, George would have preferred to be out playing with his friends, but he is now very grateful to have been given the opportunity to learn a musical instrument.

The family returned to Ireland in the mid-Seventies and George eventually teamed up with Doc Carroll and The Nightrunners. He remained with the band until they changed their name to the All-Stars and began concentrating more on Pop. Later, he formed his own band, Nashville Addition, and began playing the local pub scene in Kerry.

That arrangement could well have gone on indefinitely but for the fact that top music promoter Kieran Cavanagh heard George singing at the Rose Of Tralee Festival. Suitably impressed, he encouraged George to form the novelty James Gang with Ken Twamley. Ken was later to become known as Jesse. Within a short period, Jesse and The James Gang gained national attention with the rather controversial song, *Drop Kick Me Jesus Through The Goalposts Of Life.*

The group enjoyed considerable success until Jesse decided to move permanently to the US, leaving George to wonder what would happen next. After some thought he decided to form his own band and began recording new material.

Today, George Kane is a happy man, doing what he likes best: bringing joy and happiness to so many.

PROFILE

HOMEPLACE: *Tullamore, County Offaly*
BIRTHDAY: *September 24*
HEIGHT: *5-4*
COLOUR OF HAIR: *Black*
COLOUR OF EYES: *Brown*
ABIDING CHILDHOOD MEMORY: *My father rehearsing with his dance-band on Sunday afternoons*
EARLY AMBITIONS: *To become a pilot*
FIRST REAL JOB: *Drapery assistant*
EARLIEST RECORDING AND WHEN: *Stoney Mountain, West Virginia, 1984*
EARLY MUSICAL INFLUENCES: *Elvis Presley*
HIGHPOINT IN LIFE TO DATE: *Visiting Nashville, meeting and making new friends in the music business*
UNFULFILLED AMBITION: *To have a number one hit record*
FAVOURITE IRISH ARTISTS: *Ray Lynam, Philomena Begley*
FAVOURITE INTERNATIONAL CELEBRITIES: *Dustin Hoffman, Meryl Streep*
FAVOURITE SPORT: *Soccer*
FAVOURITE FILMS: *Rainman, The Sting*
FAVOURITE SONG OR MUSICAL ITEM: *18 Wheels And A Dozen Roses*
FAVOURITE NON-SHOWBUSINESS PASTIME: *Cooking and playing pitch and putt*
WHO WOULD YOU MOST LIKE TO MEET: *Meryl Streep*
THE QUALITY YOU MOST ADMIRE IN OTHERS: *Honesty*

STAR COMMENT

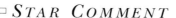

"Success in show business comes from the amount of work put into it."

SANDY KELLY

Sandy Kelly has spent her entire life in show business

Sandy Kelly has spent her entire life in show business. In fact, the Sligo-born singer has never really known any other lifestyle since making her stage debut as an assistant to a magician in her family's travelling show when she was all of three years old.

Sandy Kelly spent her formative years in Wales and became a full-time professional in her early teens. There followed a term as lead vocalist with The Fairways Showband before she teamed up with her sister, Barbara, and their cousins, Nina and Danny, to form The Duskeys. Truly a family affair, it was an enormously successful combination, and went on to represent Ireland in the Eurovision Song Contest, held in Harrogate, England, in 1982.

An extremely versatile entertainer, Sandy has the unique distinction of having represented Ireland, not only in the Eurovision Song Contest, but also in the European Gold Star Awards Final. Indeed, she won the coveted Gold Star Award, singing *Before I Met You* and the Dolly Parton composition, *I Will Always Love You*.

Yet, despite her abundant talent, Sandy seemed destined never to realise her true potential until in 1989 she signed a recording deal with K-tel and a management contract with music promoter Kieran Cavanagh. The rest, as they say, is musical history.

Sandy Kelly's excellent interpretation of the Patsy Cline hit, *Crazy*, brought her to the attention of a much wider audience, and the song richly deserved the chart success it earned. An invitation from the legendary Johnny Cash to join him in Nashville to record a duet song resulted in another inspired release, *Woodcarver*, which was recorded at the famed Bradley's Barn Studio in Nashville. Since then, Sandy has recorded more duets with Johnny Cash, appeared at the Country Music Fan Fare and The Grand Ole Opry in Nashville and guested on *Nashville Now*, a programme with an audience of millions. The latest jewel in Sandy Kelly's crown has been her hugely successful RTE television series, *Sandy*.

And so at long last Sandy Kelly is receiving the kind of recognition which is long overdue.

PROFILE

HOMEPLACE: Ballintogher, County Sligo
BIRTHDAY: February 27
HEIGHT: 5-2
COLOUR OF HAIR: Brownish
COLOUR OF EYES: Green
ABIDING CHILDHOOD MEMORY: Travelling with my family to entertain people all over Ireland; another memory is being tutored by Denis Franks and my godfather, Duskey Dan
EARLY AMBITIONS: To make records and appear on television; also to get into acting and travel the world
FIRST REAL JOB: Working as a clerk in an accountant's office in Wales; singing at night, and teaching dancing on Saturday and Sunday afternoons
EARLIEST RECORDING AND WHEN: Come Back Billy-Joe, 1976
EARLY MUSICAL INFLUENCES: The music of my family, and I loved listening to my grandmother singing. She was just amazing; people would come from miles around to hear her sing.
HIGHPOINT IN LIFE TO DATE: Recording with Johnny Cash and appearing at the Grand Ole Opry
UNFULFILLED AMBITION: To write and record my own songs
FAVOURITE IRISH ARTISTS: My sister Barbara Ellis, Matt Leavy
FAVOURITE INTERNATIONAL CELEBRITIES: Johnny Cash, Harold Bradley
FAVOURITE SPORT: None really, although I have developed an interest in soccer since watching the Irish team in the World Cup
FAVOURITE FILMS: Ben Hur, The Colour Purple
FAVOURITE SONG OR MUSICAL ITEM: The Wind Beneath My Wings
FAVOURITE NON-SHOWBUSINESS PASTIME: Going for walks with my children, William and Barbara, on the local beaches and in the forest in Sligo
WHO WOULD YOU MOST LIKE TO MEET: Mother Teresa
THE QUALITY YOU MOST ADMIRE IN OTHERS: Honesty and sincerity

STAR COMMENT

"I think we are lucky to be able to do something we truly love. Sometimes it's hard if you don't succeed, but then when you do it all seems worthwhile. The loyalty of the people who come to see us, buy our records and like what we do means ever so much. It's the best feeling in the world, so thank you!"

TONY KENNY

> **Tony Kenny grew up in the very heart of Dublin**

Versatile is the word that describes Tony Kenny's status as a professional entertainer. Tony has starred in sell-out musicals, fronted a number of bands, won a Jacobs Award for his own television series and earned chart hits in Ireland and Britain.

The British successes came about when Tony, performing under the stage name Kenny, released a number of best-selling records with Phil Coulter. In fact, one of the songs, *Heart Of Stone*, in addition to making it to number five in the British charts in 1973, also reached number one right across Europe. But at the time, Tony wasn't interested in getting too closely involved in that particular area of the business, preferring to pursue a solo career.

Tony Kenny grew up in the very heart of Dublin in the area known as the Liberties and, although initially not very interested in music, he became more and more involved because of the continual encouragement from his family and friends. The church and school choirs helped develop his skill as a vocalist, and subsequently he formed a vocal harmony group with some friends. He was just fifteen at the time. The group changed its name, eventually, to The Vampires and specialised in singing American West Coast songs. Two years later, Tony was offered the position of lead vocalist with The Sands, consisting of former members of the Miami Show-band, with musicians from the group scene. The Sands went on to become one of the most successful bands of their time with a succession of hit songs, among them *Help Me Rhonda, Dance Dance Dance, Knock Three Times* and *Candida*. The desire to make it as a solo performer prompted Tony Kenny to leave The Sands and try his luck on stage in musicals like *Jesus Christ Superstar* and *Joseph and the Amazing Technicolor Dreamcoat*. Tony Kenny has no regrets about the direction his career has taken and, in fact, for the past eight years or so he has spent six months of his working year starring in the internationally famous Jurys' Irish cabaret. It runs for the summer months in Jurys' Hotel, Dublin, and then Tony and the rest of the company take this unique flavour of Ireland across the United States.

Tony Kenny has travelled far since those early days in Dublin's Liberties.

PROFILE

HOMEPLACE: *The Liberties, Dublin City*
BIRTHDAY: *April 14*
HEIGHT: *6-2*
COLOUR OF HAIR: *Brown*
COLOUR OF EYES: *Brown*
ABIDING CHILDHOOD MEMORY: *Growing up in the heart of Dublin,*
the buzz of the city and the kind neighbours and friends
EARLY AMBITIONS: *To be in show business*
FIRST REAL JOB: *A butcher*
EARLIEST RECORDING AND WHEN: *Help Me Rhonda with*
The Sands, 1968
EARLY MUSICAL INFLUENCES: *The Beach Boys, The Four Seasons and Andy*
Williams
HIGHPOINT IN LIFE TO DATE: *Playing the lead part in Joseph and the Amazing*
Technicolour Dreamcoat to sell-out audiences all over the country
UNFULFILLED AMBITION: *I would like to visit Australia*
FAVOURITE IRISH ARTISTS: *Mary Black, Colm Wilkinson*
FAVOURITE INTERNATIONAL CELEBRITIES: *Frank Sinatra,*
Ella Fitzgerald
FAVOURITE SPORT: *Gaelic football, swimming*
FAVOURITE FILMS: *The Magnificent Seven, The Producers*
FAVOURITE SONG OR MUSICAL ITEM: *Vivaldi's The Four Seasons*
FAVOURITE NON-SHOWBUSINESS PASTIME: *Watching sport*
WHO WOULD YOU MOST LIKE TO MEET: *Frank Sinatra*
THE QUALITY YOU MOST ADMIRE IN OTHERS: *Professionalism*

STAR COMMENT

"Do your best, but, at the same time, don't take it too seriously, because at the end of the day we're all just passing through."

EILEEN KING

Ireland's Sweetheart of Country Music

*E*ileen King admits to not being particularly ambitious, yet the talented County Armagh lady has carved out a good living in the most precarious of all professions.

Eileen was born into a family of four in the little village of Camlough. Theirs was a musical household. Her mother was a good singer and her father played with a flute band in his early days. She was educated at St Mary's Intermediate School in Newry, and one of the highlights of her life there was appearing in a school opera, *The Quaker Girl*. Eileen was selected to sing in it and, as she didn't particularly like school, she was delighted to get time off for rehearsals. The two major influences in her singing career were Patsy Cline and Connie Smith, and Eileen liked nothing better than coming home from school and singing along to some of their records.

Eileen first came to the notice of the dancing public as lead vocalist with local band, The Kangaroos. Shortly afterwards Eileen was approached with a view to replacing Philomena Begley in Country Flavour. This was an offer she couldn't refuse and she spent four happy years with the band and learned a great deal about the business during that time.

Then came an invitation to start her own band which was named Country Gifts. This in turn led to an opportunity to record at the Fireside Studios in

Nashville, with such a major star as Porter Wagoner and she also appeared at the Grand Ole Opry. It was the crowning glory of Eileen's early career.

Eileen's work these days is mostly confined to the very busy British circuit but she also makes occasional appearances in Ireland. During her career Eileen King has won numerous music awards and has earned the title "Ireland's Sweetheart of Country Music".

PROFILE

HOMEPLACE: *Camlough, County Armagh*
BIRTHDAY: *August 6*
HEIGHT: *5-4*
COLOUR OF HAIR: *Brown*
COLOUR OF EYES: *Green*
ABIDING CHILDHOOD MEMORY: *Standing on a chair pretending I was singing to an audience*
EARLY AMBITIONS: *To be a singer*
FIRST REAL JOB: *Drapery assistant*
EARLIEST RECORDING AND WHEN: *Knock At My Window Tonight Love, 1974*
EARLY MUSICAL INFLUENCES: *Patsy Cline, Connie Smith*
HIGHPOINT IN LIFE TO DATE: *Recording in Nashville and appearing at Wembley*
UNFULFILLED AMBITION: *To record a live album*
FAVOURITE IRISH ARTISTS: *Brian Coll, Philomena Begley*
FAVOURITE INTERNATIONAL CELEBRITIES: *Willie Nelson, Dolly Parton*
FAVOURITE SPORT: *Not really into sport*
FAVOURITE FILMS: *Gone With The Wind, Ryan's Daughter*
FAVOURITE SONG OR MUSICAL ITEM: *The Wind Beneath My Wings*
FAVOURITE NON-SHOWBUSINESS PASTIME: *Watching TV*
WHO WOULD YOU MOST LIKE TO MEET: *Mother Teresa*
THE QUALITY YOU MOST ADMIRE IN OTHERS: *Honesty and sincerity*

STAR COMMENT

"With today's worldwide problems, I think the world is in an awful state. As far as I can see we have all become very selfish in our ways, with power and greed dominating our lives. I think it's time we all turned back to God and begin thinking of others for a change."

DOMINIC KIRWAN

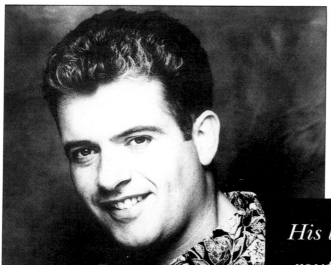

His lively dance routine adds a novelty touch to his repertoire

*D*ominic Kirwan describes himself as a balladeer whose leanings are towards the Country and Irish side of the music scene. He is from Omagh, County Tyrone, and follows in the footsteps of such noted singers from the area as Brian Coll, Philomena Begley and Frankie McBride. Furthermore, Dominic was greatly influenced by his mother, an accomplished pianist who performed regularly in local theatres and music halls.

Dominic Kirwan's introduction as a stage performer came about when he enrolled in the Seamus Kerrigan School of Irish Dancers. He was barely five years old at the time. Subsequently he began appearing as a traditional Irish dancer at festivals in England and Scotland. Indeed, at the ripe old age of twelve Dominic, then reigning Ulster minor champion, featured as one of the star attractions at a major folk festival in Norway. Interestingly, one of the highlights of Dominic's present stage act is his lively dance routine which adds a novelty touch to his wide-ranging repertoire.

In 1978 Dominic joined his first band and during the following years, although working full time as a car salesman, continued to play with many different musical combinations. All the while, however, Dominic, hoping for that elusive breakthrough, entered various talent competitions.

The formation of his present band in 1988 coincided with Dominic winning two major talent contests. The same year he recorded his debut album, *The Green Fields Of Ireland*, which received generous airplay and brought him to the attention of Ritz Records. A major recording deal followed and Dominic, in addition to releasing two hit singles, *The Green Fields Are Rolling Still* and *Oh Lonesome Me*, enjoyed considerable success with his album, *Try A Little Kindness*.

In 1990 Dominic's fourteen-track compilation, *Love Without End*, sold very well, as did his debut video, *Dominic Kirwan Live*, which was recorded at the Whitehall Theatre, Dundee, Scotland. Moreover, Dominic made a great impression when he appeared as Charley Pride's special guest during the American singer's tour of the UK in 1990.

Today Dominic Kirwan's career continues to gather momentum. The future looks bright.

PROFILE

HOMEPLACE: *Omagh, County Tyrone*
BIRTHDAY: *June 5*
HEIGHT: *5-11*
COLOUR OF HAIR: *Fair*
COLOUR OF EYES: *Blue*
ABIDING CHILDHOOD MEMORY: *Sitting on the wall outside our house crying my heart out because I didn't want to go to my first dancing class in Seamus Kerrigan's, at the age of barely five. My mother and my sister, Mary, were doing their best to persuade me, but after the first day I loved it and have no regrets.*
EARLY AMBITIONS: *To be a singer*
FIRST REAL JOB: *Storeman for car parts in O'Neill Motor Factors in Strabane*
EARLIEST RECORDING AND WHEN: *Alice Is In Wonderland, 1985*
EARLY MUSICAL INFLUENCES: *My mother and all the family, who were very musical*
HIGHPOINT IN LIFE TO DATE: *Signing a recording deal with Ritz*
UNFULFILLED AMBITION: *To have an international hit*
FAVOURITE IRISH ARTISTS: *Joe Dolan, Philomena Begley*
FAVOURITE INTERNATIONAL CELEBRITIES: *Dolly Parton, Packie Bonner*
FAVOURITE SPORT: *Gaelic football*
FAVOURITE FILMS: *Rainman, Pretty Woman*
FAVOURITE SONG OR MUSICAL ITEM: *Noreen Bán*
FAVOURITE NON-SHOWBUSINESS PASTIME: *Spending time with my friends*
WHO WOULD YOU MOST LIKE TO MEET: *Ricky Van Shelton*
THE QUALITY YOU MOST ADMIRE IN OTHERS: *Sincerity*

STAR COMMENT

"Just remember where you've come from and never forget those who have helped you along the way. It's important to be genuine and sincere and to have time for others."

MATT LEAVY

> *He has made giant strides in a relatively short period*

Matt Leavy is one of the rising stars of Irish music and, under the astute management of Kieran Cavanagh, he has made giant strides in a relatively short period. Besides appearing on various radio and television programmes, Matt played support to the legendary Buck Owens and The Buckaroos on their 1990 Irish tour. It was a major boost for the Athboy, County Meath, singer, whose entry into the mainstream of Irish music came about when he recorded a four-track cassette in Slane Studios. The cassette was sent to Bibi's programme in RTE and Matt was delighted to be invited on the show. As luck would have it, the night Matt made his television debut he met his future manager, Kieran Cavanagh, who was there with one of his stars, Sandy Kelly, and record boss Shay Hennessy of K-tel.

Kieran and Shay were mightily impressed with Matt's prowess as a vocalist and immediately offered him a management and recording contract.

Subsequently Matt recorded an excellent cassette/EP, this time under the umbrella of K-tel. The release was produced by none other than Ray Lynam and also featured Sandy Kelly on backing vocals. Matt Leavy had arrived. He had promised that if lucky enough to secure a recording contract he would launch his new record on *The Bibi Show* and sure enough that is what he did.

These days, fronting a five-piece band, Matt Leavy is fast building up a reputation as a first-rate performer, and his Neil Diamond medleys are making a huge impression with audiences of all musical persuasions.

Matt's first trip to Nashville coincided with the CMA awards and he was more than pleased to get the opportunity of seeing many of his own musical heroes, including Randy Travis, Clint Black and Ronnie Milsap. Truly a genuine Country singer.

PROFILE

HOMEPLACE: *Athboy, County Meath*
BIRTHDAY: *April 29*
HEIGHT: *6-1*
COLOUR OF HAIR: *Brown*
COLOUR OF EYES: *Blue*
ABIDING CHILDHOOD MEMORY: *Getting my first guitar*
EARLY AMBITIONS: *To be a carpenter*
FIRST REAL JOB: *Farm hand*
EARLIEST RECORDING AND WHEN: *Follow The Champions, 1987*
EARLY MUSICAL INFLUENCES: *Elvis Presley*
HIGHPOINT IN LIFE TO DATE: *Special Guest on the Buck Owen's 1990 Irish tour*
UNFULFILLED AMBITION: *To appear at the Grand Ole Opry*
FAVOURITE IRISH ARTISTS: *Chris De Burgh, Sandy Kelly*
FAVOURITE INTERNATIONAL CELEBRITIES: *Ronnie Milsap,*
Neil Diamond
FAVOURITE SPORT: *Football*
FAVOURITE FILMS: *Die Hard, Back To The Future I*
FAVOURITE SONG OR MUSICAL ITEM: *Bucks Polka*
FAVOURITE NON-SHOWBUSINESS PASTIME: *Playing pool and football*
WHO WOULD YOU MOST LIKE TO MEET: *Neil Diamond*
THE QUALITY YOU MOST ADMIRE IN OTHERS: *Hard Work*

STAR COMMENT

"It's the happiness of having music that makes my world a place worth living in."

LOGUE & McCOOL

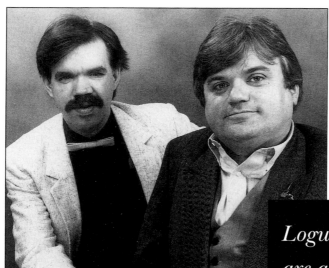

Logue & McCool are already on the high road to stardom

Not so long ago Logue & McCool were total unknowns. Today they are being talked of as one the most exciting musical combinations to emerge on the Irish music scene. What makes their achievement all the more notable is the fact that both have overcome physical handicaps to become a major Country act. Chris Logue from Ballykelly, County Derry, has been blind since birth, while Derry City-born Pat McCool contracted polio and is confined to a wheelchair.

Logue & McCool's rise to fame came directly as a result of their victory in the *Live At Three* Search For A Star competition on RTE television, where their tight harmony work and melodious vocals on their chosen song, *This Is Where The Cowboy Rides Away*, was the highlight of the talent contest. Before that breakthrough the lads had been performing as a duo, busking for the Physically Handicapped and Able Bodied Association around the streets of Belfast, Derry, Strabane and Coleraine. Consequently they were invited to appear at a number of concerts around the Belfast area.

From the very first moment he heard music, Chris Logue never wanted to be anything other than a singer. While still at school in Jordanstown Chris got his first taste of the live music scene when, at the age of fourteen, he joined a local group, Silver Partners. This lasted for two years and then

Chris left to attend Queen Alexandra College in Birmingham. While there he continued his musical interest by playing in many of the Irish clubs and bars. On returning to Ballykelly Chris re-joined Silver Partners and stayed with the group until they disbanded, whereupon he decided to try his luck as a solo artist. He was still performing as a solo singer when, in May 1989, he met Pat McCool.

Pat McCool, too, was blessed with a flair for music, especially Country. At an early age he began playing sessions with neighbours and friends in the streets near his home in the Creggan Estate in Derry. Subsequently Pat had stints with a number of local groups, including Acoustic and Trilogy. But by the time he met Chris, Pat was only playing music on a casual basis and instead was concentrating his efforts on working full time with a local charity.

Shortly after the *Live At Three* success, Logue & McCool travelled to Nashville to record their debut album which was produced by Tom Pick and Bobby Dyson at Merit Recording Studio. Simply titled *Logue & McCool*, the compilation, on the Harmac label, contained a wholesome blend of material by such artists as Merle Haggard, Marty Robbins and Willie Nelson. Among the songs included on the album are: *The Cowboy Rides Away, Shelly's Winter Love, Blue Ridge Mountain Girl, Rodeo Man, Back On My Mind Again* and *Reasons To Quit*. Not surprisingly, the album turned out to be a huge seller and earned Chris and Pat a well-deserved gold disc award. Their sixteen-track follow-up album, *Rainbow & Roses*, also produced by Tom Pick and Bobby Dyson, was another outstanding success for the talented pair.

These days Logue & McCool, under the management of Patrice, ex-Tulsa Band, front a first-rate six-piece band on the cabaret and dance-band cicruit. Logue & McCool have a distinctive style and appeal all of their own. It is safe to say they are already on the high road to stardom.

PROFILE

CHRIS LOGUE
HOMEPLACE: *Ballykelly, County Derry*
BIRTHDAY: *October 7*
HEIGHT: *5-6*
COLOUR OF HAIR: *Brown*
COLOUR OF EYES: *Blue*
ABIDING CHILDHOOD MEMORY: *The first time I heard music and I've loved it ever since*
EARLY AMBITIONS: *To sing on stage*
FIRST REAL JOB: *Singing on the pub scene*
EARLIEST RECORDING AND WHEN: *Logue & McCool album, 1990*
EARLY MUSICAL INFLUENCES: *Merle Haggard, George Jones, Charley Pride*

HIGHPOINT IN LIFE TO DATE: Getting to Nashville, appearing at Wembley
UNFULFILLED AMBITION: To meet Merle Haggard and sing with him
FAVOURITE IRISH ARTISTS: Patrice, Brian Coll
FAVOURITE INTERNATIONAL CELEBRITIES: Merle Haggard, Willie Nelson
FAVOURITE SPORT: None in particular
FAVOURITE FILMS: Hear No Evil, See No Evil, The Wizard of Oz
FAVOURITE SONG OR MUSICAL ITEM: Chill Factor (Merle Haggard)
FAVOURITE NON-SHOWBUSINESS PASTIME: Relaxing with a pint and listening to tapes
WHO WOULD YOU MOST LIKE TO MEET: Merle Haggard
THE QUALITY YOU MOST ADMIRE IN OTHERS: Honesty and sense of humour

STAR COMMENT

"Ask me to sing but don't ask me to make a comment."

PROFILE

PAT McCOOL

HOMEPLACE: Derry City
BIRTHDAY: October 14
HEIGHT: 5-00
COLOUR OF HAIR: Black going grey
COLOUR OF EYES: Blue
ABIDING CHILDHOOD MEMORY: Leaving hospital and starting primary school
EARLY AMBITIONS: To sing professionally
FIRST REAL JOB: Telephonist
EARLIEST RECORDING AND WHEN: Album for charity, 1980
EARLY MUSICAL INFLUENCES: Glen Campbell, John Denver
HIGHPOINT IN LIFE TO DATE: Recording in Nashville
UNFULFILLED AMBITION: To sing in the Grand Ole Opry
FAVOURITE IRISH ARTISTS: Mick Flavin, Susan McCann
FAVOURITE INTERNATIONAL CELEBRITIES: Merle Haggard, Glen Campbell
FAVOURITE SPORT: Football
FAVOURITE FILMS: Straw Dogs, Mad Max II
FAVOURITE SONG OR MUSICAL ITEM: Oklahoma
FAVOURITE NON-SHOWBUSINESS PASTIME: Going for long drives
WHO WOULD YOU MOST LIKE TO MEET: Merle Haggard
THE QUALITY YOU MOST ADMIRE IN OTHERS: Honesty and hard work

STAR COMMENT

"Work hard, play hard and enjoy yourself."

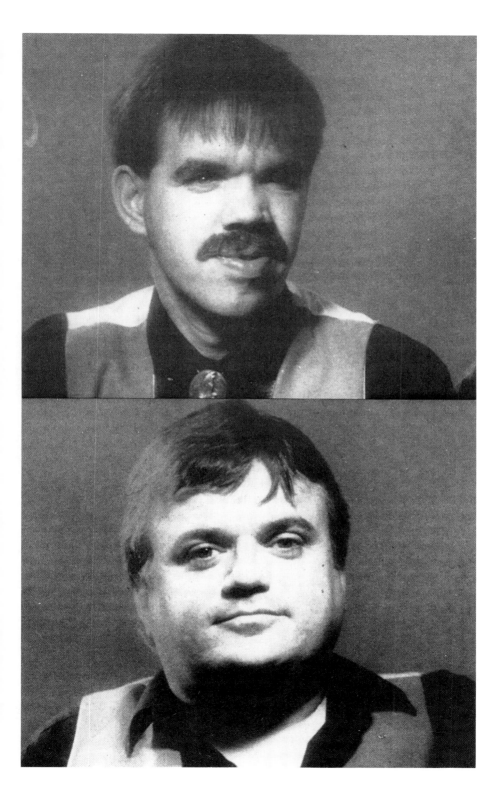

RAY LYNAM

Ray is not a man to compromise his music

*R*ay Lynam possesses one of the most authentic Country voices this side of Nashville.

Ever since he entered the mainstream of Irish music in the early Seventies Ray's immense talent has been recognised by fans of all musical persuasions, many holding the opinion that if he had concentrated his efforts more on the American than the Irish market he would now be a major international Country star. Anyone who has ever heard him sing would find it hard to disagree. Not surprisingly, over the years Ray has been consistently voted Number One Male Country Vocalist in numerous national and international polls, including *Billboard Magazine*.

Through his school years in Moate, County Westmeath, Ray Lynam played saxophone with a small local group, The Merrymen, and it was a member of that band, Kevin Sheeran, now with the Daniel O'Donnell Band, who talked him into fronting a Country band called The Hillbillies. Subsequently their recording of *Gypsy Joe And Me* proved a hugely popular release and helped launch the band on the national scene. To this day it still remains one of the songs most closely associated with The Hillbillies.

However, it was *The Selfishness Of Man* that brought Ray and the fledgling outfit their first hit, and that chart success was quickly followed by *Brand*

New Mr Me, I Can't Believe That You Stopped Loving Me, Borrowed Angel and *Second Hand Flowers*. Ray earned another stay in the Irish charts with *You're The One I Can't Live Without* and *My Elusive Dreams*, both duets with Philomena Begley.

It was always difficult to categorise the music of The Hillbillies. The band were hugely successful on the Country and Irish circuit, yet most of their recordings were influenced by American Country singers. Interestingly, one of their best-ever recordings, *I Don't Want To See Another Town* – a top twenty hit – failed to appeal to the dancing public and had to be deleted from their repertoire.

But Ray is not a man to compromise his music, refusing to change direction even if it meant having to ply his trade in a less lucrative market.

These days the Hillbillies are no more, but with the so-called "New Country" enjoying enormous popularity, Ray Lynam is singing away and is widely acclaimed as "The Boss Of New Country".

PROFILE

HOMEPLACE: *Moate, County Westmeath*
BIRTHDAY: *November 29*
HEIGHT: *6-1*
COLOUR OF HAIR: *Brown*
COLOUR OF EYES: *Blue*
ABIDING CHILDHOOD MEMORY: *Sunny days and meadows*
EARLY AMBITIONS: *To be a musician*
FIRST REAL JOB: *Musician*
EARLIEST RECORDING AND WHEN: *Busted, 1970*
EARLY MUSICAL INFLUENCES: *The music of the Sixties, Rolling Stones*
HIGHPOINT IN LIFE TO DATE: *George Jones ringing me while I was on a radio show in Nashville*
UNFULFILLED AMBITION: *To climb K 2*
FAVOURITE IRISH ARTISTS: *Mary Black, Paul Cleary*
FAVOURITE INTERNATIONAL CELEBRITIES: *Clint Eastwood, George Jones*
FAVOURITE SPORT: *Golf*
FAVOURITE FILMS: *Da!, The Spinal Tap*
FAVOURITE SONG OR MUSICAL ITEM: *I can't narrow it down as there are so many to choose from*
FAVOURITE NON-SHOWBUSINESS PASTIME: *Playing golf, reading*
WHO WOULD YOU MOST LIKE TO MEET: *Woody Allen*
THE QUALITY YOU MOST ADMIRE IN OTHERS: *Patience*

STAR COMMENT

"Silence is golden."

FRANKIE McBRIDE

> *One of the smoothest voices in the Irish music business*

*F*rom Omagh, County Tyrone, Frankie McBride has one of the smoothest voices in the Irish music business. Although Frankie grew up listening to Elvis Presley, Conway Twitty and Frankie Lane on Radio Luxembourg, it was his grandmother, Rebecca Bryden, an excellent banjo and guitar player, who exercised the greatest influence on his career. In fact, his grandmother had amassed an enormous collection of old 78s, and these helped instil in Frankie a great love of Irish music.

Frankie McBride's first theatrical interest was in pantomimes and he continued this close involvement even after he finished school and secured a job as a painter in his father's firm.

Nine years later Frankie was approached by Gerry Nugent, then manager of The Polka Dots, who invited him to join the band and share the singing duties with Brian Coll and Donald McClelland. At the time The Polka Dots were one of the major Country attractions in Ireland and Britain. Then in 1967 Frankie recorded *Five Little Fingers*, which not only reached number two in the Irish charts but also spent thirteen weeks in the British charts, peaking at number eighteen. It was an exceptional achievement and, despite the fact that he has earned chart successes with various other songs (most notably, *Burning Bridges* in 1967), Frankie will always be more closely linked with his British chart hit than any other recording. It is arguable that he never fully reaped the benefits of that hit record which could have paved the way for a breakthrough at international level. It was not to be, however, as he had just signed a contract in Ireland and felt a loyalty to the members of his band.

In recent years Frankie, in addition to recording some material in Nashville, including a duet compilation with Gloria, has continued to perform on the Irish and British circuit with considerable success.

Frankie McBride's style of singing and choice of material will always have an appreciative audience in an ever-changing music world.

PROFILE

HOMEPLACE: *Omagh, County Tyrone*
BIRTHDAY: *February 14*
HEIGHT: *5-11*
COLOUR OF HAIR: *Brown*
COLOUR OF EYES: *Hazel*
ABIDING CHILDHOOD MEMORY: *Spending my summer holidays at my grandparents' farm in Gorthannigan, which is situated between Newtownstewart and Omagh*
EARLY AMBITIONS: *To be a singer*
FIRST REAL JOB: *Painting and decorating with my father*
EARLIEST RECORDING AND WHEN: *One For The Road, 1965/66*
EARLY MUSICAL INFLUENCES: *Jim Reeves, Brook Benton*
HIGHPOINT IN LIFE TO DATE: *Five Little Fingers entering the British charts*
UNFULFILLED AMBITION: *To have a number one hit in Ireland*
FAVOURITE IRISH ARTISTS: *Joe Dolan, Louise Morrissey*
FAVOURITE INTERNATIONAL CELEBRITIES: *Terry Wogan, Jack Nicholson*
FAVOURITE SPORT: *Football*
FAVOURITE FILMS: *One Flew Over The Cuckoo's Nest, Midnight Express*
FAVOURITE SONG OR MUSICAL ITEM: *Forty Shades Of Green*
FAVOURITE NON-SHOWBUSINESS PASTIME: *Fishing*
WHO WOULD YOU MOST LIKE TO MEET: *Terry Wogan*
THE QUALITY YOU MOST ADMIRE IN OTHERS: *Honesty and integrity*

STAR COMMENT

"To be happy and healthy."

FRANK MCCAFFREY

He is recognised as a star in his own right

*F*rank McCaffrey is a man at peace with himself. Contented and easy going, the Westport-born singer has a voice to match the very best. Born the second youngest of eight into a family with a rich musical tradition – his grandfather, Peter McConville, was the master of the local Brass Band – Frank began his musical journey when barely eight years old by teaming up with his grandfather. To this day Frank keeps his links with the Brass Band which he holds in high esteem, acknowledging that it was very beneficial, not just to himself, but to countless others in the music business.

While still at school Frank joined local band, The Beat Minstrels, owned at the time by Basil Morahan, who is better known nowadays as Dan The Street Singer. From there Frank eventually moved on to The Friel Men, another local outfit with whom he gained valuable stage experience by playing support to many of the more established showbands of the day. After leaving school, he was offered a position with Country Folk which had the legendary Margo as their lead vocalist, and when Margo was hospitalised as a result of a car accident Frank moved up to lead singer.

In this role he recorded his first album, *Introducing Frank McCaffrey*, containing such perennial favourites as: *Eileen, Shall My Soul Pass Through Old Ireland, Coastline Of Mayo, Rose Marie* and *Faded Love*.

Around the time of the decline of the ballroom scene Frank left the Country Folk line-up to front the newly formed Band Of Gold. Feeling that the time was right to concentrate on cabaret, he signed with Ritz Records and embarked on concert tours with Philomena Begley.

While Frank has played support in his time to many of the big name stars, including Foster & Allen, Joe Dolan and Brendan Shine, nowadays he is recognised as a star in his own right, regularly fronting concerts in Britain and elsewhere.

PROFILE

HOMEPLACE: *Westport, County Mayo*
BIRTHDAY: *January 14*
HEIGHT: *6-1*
COLOUR OF HAIR: *Black*
COLOUR OF EYES: *Blue*
ABIDING CHILDHOOD MEMORY: *Going to a dance when I was only twelve or thirteen and shouldn't have been there at all. I remember looking up at the band playing and thinking, whatever they're doing it must be heaven.*
EARLY AMBITIONS: *To be a musician*
FIRST REAL JOB: *Assistant storeman in a garage*
EARLIEST RECORDING AND WHEN: *Introducing Frank McCaffrey album, 1976*
EARLY MUSICAL INFLUENCES: *My grandfather, Peter McConville and The Beatles*
HIGHPOINT IN LIFE TO DATE: *Playing support to Big Jim Farley and his band in The Travellers Friend, Castlebar, County Mayo. I was with The Friel Men at the time and afterwards Jim invited me on stage to sing two songs. It meant a great deal to me at the time.*
UNFULFILLED AMBITION: *No major ambitions; although I would like to write a hit song*
FAVOURITE IRISH ARTISTS: *Philomena Begley and Joe Dolan*
FAVOURITE INTERNATIONAL CELEBRITIES: *Pat Jennings, Kenny Dalglish*
FAVOURITE SPORT: *Squash*
FAVOURITE FILMS: *The Good, The Bad and The Ugly, The Music Lovers*
FAVOURITE SONG OR MUSICAL ITEM: *Imagine*
FAVOURITE NON-SHOWBUSINESS PASTIME: *Fishing*
WHO WOULD YOU MOST LIKE TO MEET: *Willie Nelson*
THE QUALITY YOU MOST ADMIRE IN OTHERS: *Understanding*

STAR COMMENT

"It's nice to have good health and give others, who aren't as fortunate, a helping hand. And don't let yourself be blinded by ambition."

JIM McCANN

One of Ireland's most prominent balladeers

*B*ut for the fact that music got in the way, Jim McCann would probably now be a doctor. At the age of seventeen Jim became a medical student at UCD while at the same time playing with various bands, including The Boston Showband, Bob Ormsby's All Stars, and The Nashvilles. Consequently the medical studies were neglected, and Jim headed off to England for the summer, where he secured employment in Birds custard factory in Birmingham.

It was while overseas that he developed a keen interest in folk music, as a way of socialising with other Irish emigrants. When Jim returned to Ireland at Christmas 1965 he replaced Paddy Roche in The Ludlows, then acknowledged as Ireland's most popular folk trio. A few months later the group had an enormous hit with *The Sea Around Us* which enjoyed a lengthy stay at the top of the Irish charts. More hits followed, thanks to such songs as *The Wind Thru The Rafters* and *Enniskillen Dragoons*.

Jim McCann left the Ludlows in 1967 and joined the cast of Maureen Potter's *Gaels Of Laughter* in the Gaiety Theatre. Around that time every few months seemed to bring a change or two in his life. He returned to the folk scene, alternating between Ireland and England, then joined the first Irish production of *Jesus Christ Superstar* before moving on as narrator in the successful production of *Joseph and the Amazing Technicolor Dreamcoat*. Then in 1974 Jim teamed up with The Dubliners and for the next five years he toured extensively with them.

One of Ireland's most prominent balladeers, Jim McCann was born in Dublin but spent his early years in Donegal town. Later the family (his father was a schools inspector) moved to Tuam, County Galway and then back again to Dublin where Jim attended Terenure College.

During his varied career Jim McCann has hosted several television series and in addition has recorded a number of hits, including *Her Father Didn't Like Me Anyway, Alone, Easy and Slow, Love's Old Sweet Song* and, his biggest ever single success, *Grace*, a poignant song which tells about the marriage of Grace Gifford and Joseph Mary Plunkett.

Jim McCann loves to sing and that he does with great style.

PROFILE

HOMEPLACE: Dublin City
BIRTHDAY: October 26
HEIGHT: 5-9½
COLOUR OF HAIR: Fair
COLOUR OF EYES: Blue
ABIDING CHILDHOOD MEMORY: Diving off the pier at Keel in Achill, County Mayo, and landing on a huge basking shark which was tied up to the jetty. I didn't know the shark was dead and my family tell me that I almost ran along the surface of the water with the fright. I was about ten or eleven at the time.
EARLY AMBITIONS: To be a singer
FIRST REAL JOB: Working in Roches Chemist in O'Connell St, Dublin
EARLIEST RECORDING AND WHEN: The Sea Around Us, 1966
EARLY MUSICAL INFLUENCES: Buddy Holly, Eddie Cochrane
HIGHPOINT IN LIFE TO DATE: Singing the National Anthem in Irish before the Seán Mannion – Mike McCallum World Title fight in Madison Square Garden, New York
UNFULFILLED AMBITION: To have an international hit record
FAVOURITE IRISH ARTISTS: Joe Dolan, Maureen Potter
FAVOURITE INTERNATIONAL CELEBRITIES: Peter Ustinov, Bette Midler
FAVOURITE SPORT: Golf
FAVOURITE FILMS: The Godfather, The Producers
FAVOURITE SONG OR MUSICAL ITEM: David Gates Bread album
FAVOURITE NON-SHOWBUSINESS PASTIME: Cooking
WHO WOULD YOU MOST LIKE TO MEET: Tom Sharpe
THE QUALITY YOU MOST ADMIRE IN OTHERS: Sense of Humour

STAR COMMENT

"I would wish to see an end to the despicable practice of innocent people being kidnapped for political ends; and a quick and equitable end to the troubles in my own country."

SUSAN McCANN

Susan was the first European singer to be invited to Dollywood

*I*nternational singing star Susan McCann is one of Ireland's most highly rated entertainers. Her reputation as a quality singer is acknowledged by many leading Nashville superstars and she has appeared on numerous occasions at the Grand Ole Opry. Susan has also performed in New York's Carnegie Hall and the Royal Albert Hall, London. One of the highlights of her remarkably successful career was her proud victory in the European Gold Star Awards final in 1982.

As a teenager in Forkhill, County Armagh, Susan sang with the local John Murphy Country Céilí band. While with the band she met her future husband, musician Dennis Heaney. Both of them felt that working with the band did not give them the kind of security they needed for a married life, and so Dennis began to study and qualified as an accountant while Susan trained for a career as a hairdresser. They didn't quite desert the music scene, though, and formed their own three-piece band, called The Fairylanders. However, it was not until after the birth of their two children, Brendan and Linda, that Susan decided to adopt a more businesslike approach to her career by signing a contract with Top Spin Records.

Shortly after turning professional in the mid-Seventies, Susan McCann's recording of a tribute song, *Big Tom Is Still The King*, reached number one in the Irish charts. That was the beginning, and since then Susan has enjoyed unprecedented success.

In recognition of her status as a major Country star, Susan, who now lives in Newry, was the first European singer to be invited to Dollywood, Dolly Parton's famous entertainment centre near Knoxville, Tennessee, for a Country Music Spectacular. Susan was also the first non-American artist to headline the famous Strawberry Festival in Tampa, Florida. That important milestone occurred in 1991. Before that, though, in 1990 she signed a major contract with the internationally renowned Prism Leisure Company and that organisation now looks after all her promotional and recording matters in the UK.

Throughout her career Susan McCann has always recorded first-rate material, gaining Irish chart success on numerous occasions, most notably with *Big Tom Is Still The King, Rockabilly Can Rock, While I Was Making Love To You, When The Sun Says Goodbye To The Mountain, Broken Speed Of The Sound Of Loneliness* and her most recent hit, *String Of Diamonds*.

Susan McCann has made an invaluable contribution to Country music and will surely remain a star attraction on the international scene.

PROFILE

HOMEPLACE: *Carrickasticken, Forkhill, County Armagh*
BIRTHDAY: *February 26*
HEIGHT: *5-4*
COLOUR OF HAIR: *Auburn*
COLOUR OF EYES: *Brown*
ABIDING CHILDHOOD MEMORY: *On my sixth birthday, my father – and I can still see him in his working clothes – presented me with a quarter of sweets. It was a real treat. He lifted me up in his arms and sang "Happy Birthday" while I reminded him that I was now very old. "Yes you are," I remember him saying, "you really are old, you are six years of age".*
EARLY AMBITIONS: *To be a singer*
FIRST REAL JOB: *Shop assistant*
EARLIEST RECORDING AND WHEN: *Feelin' Single, Seeing Double, 1976*
EARLY MUSICAL INFLUENCES: *Patsy Cline*
HIGHPOINT IN LIFE TO DATE: *Being invited to present a show called She's Got It on RTE television*
UNFULFILLED AMBITION: *To have a number one in the British charts*
FAVOURITE IRISH ARTISTS: *Joe Dolan, Mary Black*
FAVOURITE INTERNATIONAL CELEBRITIES: *Dolly Parton, Kenny Rogers*
FAVOURITE SPORT: *None really*
FAVOURITE FILMS: *Madame X, The Sound Of Music*
FAVOURITE SONG OR MUSICAL ITEM: *Edelweiss*
FAVOURITE NON-SHOWBUSINESS PASTIME: *Relaxing on the family farm away from it all*
WHO WOULD YOU MOST LIKE TO MEET: *President Gorbachev*
THE QUALITY YOU MOST ADMIRE IN OTHERS: *Loyalty*

STAR COMMENT

"I long for peace in our country and wish health and happiness for everyone."

JOHNNY McEVOY

A natural storyteller, Johnny McEvoy has written numerous songs

Johnny McEvoy, ace singer songwriter, has been an integral part of Irish show business for over a quarter of a century.

In 1966, singing with the fervour of a supreme balladeer, he raced to the top of the Irish charts with his rousing version of *Mursheen Durkin*. As is often the case, what appeared to have been an overnight breakthrough was in fact the culmination of many years of hard work and dedication. Previously, Johnny had been performing on the folk circuit and was a regular at fleadhanna ceoil throughout the country.

Following his chart success, Johnny toured extensively, taking in the US, Canada and the UK. His reputation was further enhanced when he had two other chart hits, *Boston Burglar* in 1967, and a year later that perennial favourite, *Nora*.

A natural storyteller, Johnny McEvoy has written numerous songs, many widely admired as masterful; among these are: *Long Before Your Time* (a number one in 1976), *Rich Man's Garden, You Seldom Come To See Me Anymore* and *Michael*, one of his most recent chart hits. By composing and recording the song about Michael Collins, Johnny fulfilled a lifelong ambition because he had greatly admired the Big Fellow. For his own television programme, in the RTE series *My Ireland*, Johnny also wrote *The Ballad of John Williams*, a rather poignant song which tells of a young couple who set sail from Cobh on the ill-fated Titanic.

Keeping up with changing music trends, Johnny, nowadays managed by Noel Carty, formed his own band in the early Seventies and he has since continued to perform on the cabaret and ballroom circuit with considerable success.

For Johnny McEvoy, "it's not the miles you travel but the stops you make along the way". Thankfully, in Johnny's case, every stop brings a song or two and that is another reason why this gifted balladeer has remained at the peak of his profession for so many years.

PROFILE

HOMEPLACE: Banagher, County Offaly
BIRTHDAY: April 24
HEIGHT: 5-8
COLOUR OF HAIR: Black going grey
COLOUR OF EYES: Amber
ABIDING CHILDHOOD MEMORY: The many summers spent in grandmother's
house in Clonfert, County Galway, saving the hay, cutting
the turf and making the tea in the bog. I also remember sitting in the
house listening to stories in front of the open fire.
EARLY AMBITIONS: To become a priest
FIRST REAL JOB: Apprentice fitter
EARLIEST RECORDING AND WHEN: Today Is The Highway, 1965
EARLY MUSICAL INFLUENCES: The Weavers, Pete Seeger,
Rambling Jack Elliot and Hank Williams
HIGHPOINT IN LIFE TO DATE: The night Mursheen Durkin went to number one
in the Irish charts
UNFULFILLED AMBITION: To have a number one hit in Britain
FAVOURITE IRISH ARTISTS: Dolores Keane, Joe Dolan
FAVOURITE INTERNATIONAL CELEBRITIES: President Gorbachev,
Neil Diamond
FAVOURITE SPORT: Hurling
FAVOURITE FILMS: Close Encounters, Doctor Zhivago
FAVOURITE SONG OR MUSICAL ITEM: If Wishes Were Fishes
FAVOURITE NON-SHOWBUSINESS PASTIME: Reading history books
WHO WOULD YOU MOST LIKE TO MEET: Neil Armstrong
THE QUALITY YOU MOST ADMIRE IN OTHERS: Trustworthiness

STAR COMMENT

"I have great admiration for people who go out to help others who are much less well off, and for no personal gain give up a comfortable life of their own."

SEAMUS MCGEE

Seamus McGee helping to maintain the proud musical tradition of County Donegal

Gweedore, County Donegal singer, Seamus McGee, has more than a home-place in common with members of the internationally renowned group, Clannad. Seamus was taught to play piano and accordion by Leo Brennan, father of Máire Ní Bhraonáin and Enya, of *Orinoco Flow* fame, and his primary schoolteacher, Master Duggan, is the father of Noel and Patrick, both of whom are members of Clannad.

Despite these early musical influences, however, Seamus McGee had no intention of pursuing a full-time career in the music business. Instead, his sights were firmly fixed on joining his father's successful building firm. In fact, it was with this in mind that Seamus decided to repeat his Leaving Certificate in an attempt to gain honours in drawing. Ironically, he was back at school only a month when he was approached by Cyril Curran, then manager of The Nashville Showband, who offered him the position of lead vocalist with the band. Cyril had seen Seamus perform at Hudie Beags in Gweedore and was very impressed with the young singer's talent. Seamus decided to forego his studies and opted instead to try his luck on the music circuit for the following three years, before he secured a job in GT Carpets in Gweedore.

For the next eight years Seamus, in his capacity as technical manager, travelled the world and enjoyed every minute of it. Indeed, but for the fact that the factory closed down in 1979 due to the recession, he might never have gone back to the professional music circuit. After the closure of the factory Seamus worked with his father for a few years, but, encouraged by his friends, he formed his own band in the mid-Eighties. His debut EP release, featuring such numbers as *Donegal Shore* and *Tonight Mary Ann*, received generous airplay and did much to establish his name on the national music scene. Since then Seamus, as well as playing at all the major dance venues, has appeared on many of the most popular television shows. In addition, he enjoyed Irish chart success with *Come Home Danny Boy* which, incidentally, was co-written by Seamus and his former sound operator, Danny O'Donnell.

Certainly, Seamus McGee is playing his part in helping to maintain the proud musical tradition of County Donegal.

PROFILE

HOMEPLACE: *Gweedore, County Donegal*
BIRTHDAY: *December 11*
HEIGHT: *5-8*
COLOUR OF HAIR: *Brown*
COLOUR OF EYES: *Blue*
ABIDING CHILDHOOD MEMORY: *Learning to play musical instruments with Noel Duggan in his own home, at the age of about ten; I have fond memories of those early days*
EARLY AMBITIONS: *To be a building contractor*
FIRST REAL JOB: *Lead vocalist with The Nashville Showband*
EARLIEST RECORDING AND WHEN: *Accidentally On Purpose EP, 1984*
EARLY MUSICAL INFLUENCES: *Jim Reeves*
HIGHPOINT IN LIFE TO DATE: *Receiving a standing ovation when I sang Come Home Danny Boy at the 1989 Peterborough Festival*
UNFULFILLED AMBITION: *To have a number one hit in the Irish charts*
FAVOURITE IRISH ARTISTS: *Mick Flavin, Sandy Kelly*
FAVOURITE INTERNATIONAL CELEBRITIES: *Enya, Randy Travis*
FAVOURITE SPORT: *Gaelic football*
FAVOURITE FILMS: *Any of the "Death Wish" films*
FAVOURITE SONG OR MUSICAL ITEM: *He'll Have To Go*
FAVOURITE NON-SHOWBUSINESS PASTIME: *Going to the cinema, dancing*
WHO WOULD YOU MOST LIKE TO MEET: *Clint Eastwood*
THE QUALITY YOU MOST ADMIRE IN OTHERS: *Personality*

STAR COMMENT

"If at first you don't succeed, try and try again."

M A R G O

A voice unlike any other in the music business

*M*argo O'Donnell, as much a part of the Irish entertainment scene as the mountains and rivers are part of her beloved Donegal, will always command a special place in the hearts of Country and Irish music lovers. Blessed with an instantly recognisable voice – a voice unlike any other in the music business – Margo has remained a star attraction for well over twenty-five years. Equally important is the fact that she has always maintained a close relationship with her fans, as loyal a following as can be found anywhere. Margo's greatest attribute as a singer, however, is her special ability to interpret a song and perform it with genuine feeling. Nowhere is that talent more in evidence than in the poignant song, *The Emigrant,* featured on a recent album, *Trip Through Ireland.* In what is an inspired performance, Margo conveys the pain and loneliness of the old man who is the subject of the song. Known affectionately as "The Queen Of Country and Irish", Margo is a highly accomplished entertainer whose enthusiasm is as infectious as ever.

Margo's road to musical fame began in the late Sixties when she joined a local group, The Keynotes, while still at school in Donegal. Irish chart success followed rapidly with *Bonny Irish Boy* and *Road By The River,* a number two in 1968. Some time later she left The Keynotes to front her own band, Country Folk, and almost immediately raced to the top of the charts with an old Irish ballad, *I'll Forgive And I'll Try To Forget*. A serious car accident in the mid-Seventies kept her off the road for over a year, but happily Margo returned to team up with Larry Cunningham for a duet chart hit, *Hello Mr Peters*.

Through the years Margo's recordings have continued to reflect her love of Country and Irish music, and to her credit she has never strayed from her early influences. Besides recording numerous best-selling albums and singles, Margo's substantial list of major achievements have included appearances at Carnegie Hall, New York, and The Royal Albert Hall, London, plus her very own RTE television series which proved enormously successful. Margo makes no secret of her great affection for her home-place, Kincasslagh, where she was honoured in 1989 in recognition of her twenty-five years in show business. What made the occasion all the more special for Margo was that her younger brother, Daniel O'Donnell, made an unexpected appearance on what was a memorable night. Indeed, nothing has pleased Margo more than the tremendous success Daniel has achieved in recent years.

Margo still gets immense satisfaction from performing and recording and is looking forward to conquering pastures new in the years ahead. A special and unique Country and Irish singer.

PROFILE

HOMEPLACE: *Kincasslagh, County Donegal*
BIRTHDAY: *February 6*
HEIGHT: *5-5*
COLOUR OF HAIR: *Brown*
COLOUR OF EYES: *Blue/Grey*
ABIDING CHILDHOOD MEMORY: *Visiting my grandparents on*
Owey Island off the coast of Donegal
EARLY AMBITIONS: *I've been singing all my life, so to be honest I've never really had*
time to think about ambitions
FIRST REAL JOB: *Potato picking in Scotland*
EARLIEST RECORDING AND WHEN: *Bonny Irish Boy/Dear God, 1968*
EARLY MUSICAL INFLUENCES: *Patsy Cline*
HIGHPOINT IN LIFE TO DATE: *Anniversary celebration of my*
twenty-five years in show business in Kincasslagh Hall, Donegal
UNFULFILLED AMBITION: *To record in Nashville*
FAVOURITE IRISH ARTISTS: *Daniel O'Donnell, Maisie McDaniel*
FAVOURITE INTERNATIONAL CELEBRITIES: *Chris Evert, George Jones*
FAVOURITE SPORT: *Tennis*
FAVOURITE FILMS: *Love Story, The Ten Commandments*
FAVOURITE SONG OR MUSICAL ITEM: *Dear God*
FAVOURITE NON-SHOWBUSINESS PASTIME: *Reading*
WHO WOULD YOU MOST LIKE TO MEET: *Mother Teresa*
THE QUALITY YOU MOST ADMIRE IN OTHERS: *Honesty*

STAR COMMENT

"Keep your head very level, and stay away from the drink at all costs."

LOUISE MORRISSEY

Louise became an instant success with Country music fans

Snging comes as second nature to "The Bansha Lass", Louise Morrissey. Her father was a member of a local band and doubtless this helped to encourage a love of all things musical in the young Louise.

On leaving school Louise spent some time working as a hairdresser in her native Tipperary. But the inevitable happened and music became the young girl's main interest, prompting her to join brothers Billy and Norman in The Morrisseys Folk Group. In time The Morrisseys became a major attraction on the concert and cabaret scene. They sang together for some years until 1988, when they decided that a change of style to Country and Irish was advisable, although Louise herself was a little apprehensive about the prospects of fronting a bigger band on the Country circuit.

There was no need to worry because, when her flair for Country music became apparent, Louise became an instant success with Country music fans. Shortly after its release her second Country offering, *The Night Daniel O'Donnell Came To Town*, made it into the Irish charts. The song was a play on an old Johnny Cash hit, *The Night Hank Williams Came To Town*, and it was specifically rewritten for Louise by Tipperary songwriter, Nick McCarthy. Although a novelty recording, the song received generous airplay and helped consolidate Louise Morrissey's reputation as a Country singer of considerable ability. In 1988 Louise was voted Favourite Female Vocalist of the Year by the readers of the *RTE Guide*. Then in 1990 Louise Morrissey, singing an Irish song, *Tipperary On My Mind*, composed by Nick McCarthy, finished ahead of fourteen other countries to claim the prestigious European Gold Star Award. It was a well-deserved achievement. In fact 1990 turned out to be quite a year for Louise as she also won the National Rehab Country Music Award for the first time.

The transition from Folk to Country has been an unqualified success for Louise Morrissey, one of the most versatile entertainers in Ireland today.

PROFILE

HOMEPLACE: Bansha, County Tipperary
BIRTHDAY: March 23
HEIGHT: 5-3
COLOUR OF HAIR: Brown
COLOUR OF EYES: Green
ABIDING CHILDHOOD MEMORY: Living in the old family house in Bansha;
collecting the eggs from the hens at the age of about four and
breaking most of them when I'd fall
EARLY AMBITIONS: To be an air hostess
FIRST REAL JOB: Trainee hairdresser
EARLIEST RECORDING AND WHEN: Farewell To Carlingford, 1978
EARLY MUSICAL INFLUENCES: The Brannigans, The Pattersons
HIGHPOINT IN LIFE TO DATE: Singing Slievenamon in Croke Park during the
1988 All-Ireland Hurling Final between Galway and Tipperary; I'll never forget the
atmosphere in Croke Park that day. It was wonderful,
too, playing to a worldwide television audience of millions.
UNFULFILLED AMBITION: To be very successful in Britain and Australia
FAVOURITE IRISH ARTISTS: Ray Lynam, Philomena Begley
FAVOURITE INTERNATIONAL CELEBRITIES: Emmylou Harris,
The Judds
FAVOURITE SPORT: Hurling
FAVOURITE FILMS: Stir Crazy, Star Wars
FAVOURITE SONG OR MUSICAL ITEM: Mr Bojangles
FAVOURITE NON-SHOWBUSINESS PASTIME: Walking in the countryside
WHO WOULD YOU MOST LIKE TO MEET: Randy Travis
THE QUALITY YOU MOST ADMIRE IN OTHERS: Sincerity

STAR COMMENT

"Anyone wanting to get on in life must be prepared to work hard and keep
a good head on their shoulders."

J O E   M U R R A Y

Joe Murray has achieved a great deal in a remarkably short time

*F*rom apprentice mechanic to lead vocalist: in Joe Murray's case that transition happened literally overnight. Joe was employed at a garage in his native County Monaghan when proprietor Peter Carbin came up with the idea of forming a Country music band and Joe was chosen as lead vocalist. That was the first step in a career which has seen him emerge from total obscurity to national prominence in the space of a few short years.

Not long afterwards Joe and his fellow-musicians released a four-track cassette called *Wild Flowers*, which proved to be a major turning point in his career. Kevin McCooey, manager of the legendary Big Tom, heard the tape and came along to see the Scotstown youngster perform live. He was suitably impressed and lost no time in offering eighteen-year-old Joe the position of lead vocalist with The Travellers, replacing no less a figure than Big Tom himself. It was an opportunity of a lifetime and so on 2 June 1989, in the Glencairn Hotel, Castleblayney, Joe Murray fronted the Travellers for the very first time. It was an occasion he's unlikely to ever forget.

The next step was the release of a promotional single, the Don Gibson composition, *Blue Blue Day*, which helped to introduce Joe Murray's vocal talents to a much wider audience. Since then Joe has featured on a number of television programmes, including *The Daniel O'Donnell Show, Kenny Live, The Bibi Show* and *Live At Three.*

The last year or so has been very exciting for Joe Murray, with extensive touring at home and abroad, plus his Top Ten success with the Michael Godfrey-penned number, *The Tender Years*, which, not surprisingly, is also the title of his debut fourteen-track CD.

In a notoriously difficult and uncertain business, Joe Murray has achieved a great deal in a remarkably short time.

PROFILE

HOMEPLACE: Scotstown, County Monaghan
BIRTHDAY: April 12
HEIGHT: 5-7
COLOUR OF HAIR: Sandy
COLOUR OF EYES: Blue
ABIDING CHILDHOOD MEMORY: Looking forward to relatives coming home for Christmas; that was always very special in our house
EARLY AMBITIONS: To be a mechanic
FIRST REAL JOB: Apprentice mechanic
EARLIEST RECORDING AND WHEN: Wild Flowers, 1989
EARLY MUSICAL INFLUENCES: Charley Pride, Ricky Skaggs
HIGHPOINT IN LIFE TO DATE: Becoming lead vocalist with The Travellers
UNFULFILLED AMBITION: To write a hit song
FAVOURITE IRISH ARTISTS: Sandy Kelly, John Hogan
FAVOURITE INTERNATIONAL CELEBRITIES: Emmylou Harris, Johnny Cash
FAVOURITE SPORT: Golf
FAVOURITE FILMS: The Good, The Bad and The Ugly, Dirty Harry
FAVOURITE SONG OR MUSICAL ITEM: Tender Years
FAVOURITE NON-SHOWBUSINESS PASTIME: Swimming, golf
WHO WOULD YOU MOST LIKE TO MEET: Pope John Paul II
THE QUALITY YOU MOST ADMIRE IN OTHERS: Honesty

STAR COMMENT

"Be nice to everyone on your way up, you'll need them again coming down."

DECLAN NERNEY

He performed two songs during the half-time interval at the 1990 All-Ireland Football Final

*F*rom the time he first won a prize for performing a song and recitation on the famed McFaddens Travelling Show there was never any doubt in Declan Nerney's mind as to where his future lay. He was just five years old at the time.

Subsequently the purchase of a guitar, which he taught himself to play, ensured that when the time came to enter the professional ranks he was ideally prepared to take up a position with Paddy Hanrahan and The Oklahoma. That was in 1972.

Later Declan joined the Hi-Lows Showband and remained with the band for about a year before becoming a valued member of Gene Stuart's newly formed band, The Homesteaders. For six years Declan travelled the country with what was then acknowledged as one of Ireland's leading outfits.

Declan left in 1980 and teamed up with Brian Coll who, he readily admits, encouraged him to try his luck as a solo performer. It proved to be a wise decision and within a short period Declan, displaying all the attributes of an experienced performer, rapidly emerged as a singer to be reckoned with on the Country and Irish music scene. His debut cassette tape, *Picture Of My World*, turned out to be among the top-selling Irish compilations of that year.

Under the guiding influence of his manager, Frank Kilbride, Declan Nerney's career has really taken flight in the last eighteen months with appearances at both the Wembley and Roundwood Park Festivals, and he performed two songs during the half-time interval at the 1990 All-Ireland Football Final, which was transmitted worldwide. He has also earned deserved chart success, most notably with the popular favourite, *If The World Turned Into Ashes* and the catchy numbers, *Never Again Will I Knock On Your Door* and *The Marquee In Drumlish*, all of which he arranged and produced himself.

The multi-talented Drumlish man, renowned for his live performances, has clearly established himself as an entertainer of some considerable merit.

PROFILE

HOMEPLACE: *Drumlish, County Longford*
BIRTHDAY: *May 20*
HEIGHT: *5-4*
COLOUR OF HAIR: *Black*
COLOUR OF EYES: *Green*
ABIDING CHILDHOOD MEMORY: *School Around The Corner with Paddy Crosbie*
EARLY AMBITIONS: *To become a musician*
FIRST REAL JOB: *Lead guitarist with Paddy Hanrahan and The Oklahoma*
EARLIEST RECORDING AND WHEN: *Heartaches By The Number, 1975*
EARLY MUSICAL INFLUENCES: *Jim Reeves and The Beatles*
HIGHPOINT IN LIFE TO DATE: *Appearing at the Wembley International Country Music Festival*
UNFULFILLED AMBITION: *To get married*
FAVOURITE IRISH ARTISTS: *Brian Coll, Philomena Begley*
FAVOURITE INTERNATIONAL CELEBRITIES: *Stevie Wonder, Bruce Forsyth*
FAVOURITE SPORT: *Gaelic football*
FAVOURITE FILMS: *One Flew Over The Cuckoo's Nest, The Quiet Man*
FAVOURITE SONG OR MUSICAL ITEM: *I Love You Because*
FAVOURITE NON-SHOWBUSINESS PASTIME: *Spending time with my friends*
WHO WOULD YOU MOST LIKE TO MEET: *Pope John Paul II*
THE QUALITY YOU MOST ADMIRE IN OTHERS: *Good humour*

STAR COMMENT
"Whatever you do, keep smiling."

MICHAEL O'BRIEN

The genial Clare singer has built up a loyal and appreciative following

*T*he spectacular success of his debut single, *The Veil Of White Lace*, and the subsequent screening of a television documentary about his lifestyle, gave Michael O'Brien his first real break in the music business.

All this happened after Michael released an album featuring some of his own material, plus a selection of well-known numbers. Although he was unaware of it at the time, it was to prove the turning point in his career. Ironically, it was *The Veil Of White Lace*, included on his album at the last minute to fill a gap, that became the major Irish hit of the year. At the time Michael was also working as a male nurse, and it was this unique combination that prompted producer Paul Cusack to film a documentary about his way of life which proved an overwhelming success on RTE television.

Shortly afterwards Michael opted for a full-time career in show business, although the talented singer hasn't quite ruled out the possibility of a return to the nursing profession, perhaps at some future date.

Born the youngest of five in Bodyke, County Clare, Michael had an intense longing to get involved in some area of show business from a very early age. In fact, he was so determined to get a guitar that when no one was prepared to buy one for him he decided to make one himself. That came about as a result of his flair for carpentry, a craft in which he still maintains a great interest.

With many big-selling singles and albums to his credit, Michael broke new ground in the summer of 1990 by recording his first video, *An Evening With Michael O'Brien*, in the John Player Theatre, in Dublin. The music world is filled with countless stories of talents going undiscovered and gifted entertainers failing to win the recognition their talent deserves. Even though it took him many years to reach the higher echelons of the music business, Michael O'Brien does not complain. Since his career took flight, the genial Clare singer has consolidated his position as a first-rate Country singer, and thanks to his relaxed style and wide musical repertoire has built up a loyal and appreciative following.

PROFILE

HOMEPLACE: *Coolreagh, Bodyke, County Clare*
BIRTHDAY: *June 28*
HEIGHT: *5-7*
COLOUR OF HAIR: *Brown*
COLOUR OF EYES: *Blue*
ABIDING CHILDHOOD MEMORY: *My mother suffered greatly with arthritis and I can never remember when she wasn't in pain. I always felt helpless that I was unable to do anything to help her ease the pain. Sadly, because of her illness, my mother died in the early Seventies.*
EARLY AMBITIONS: *To be a nurse*
FIRST REAL JOB: *Working in a piano factory in Shannon*
EARLIEST RECORDING AND WHEN: *The Cliffs Of Moher album, 1985*
EARLY MUSICAL INFLUENCES: *My father, Hank Locklin, Jim Reeves and local singers and musicians*
HIGHPOINT IN LIFE TO DATE: *Playing to a crowd upwards of 100,000 in the London Irish Festival at Roundwood in 1987*
UNFULFILLED AMBITION: *To record in Nashville*
FAVOURITE IRISH ARTISTS: *Louise Morrissey, Mick Flavin*
FAVOURITE INTERNATIONAL CELEBRITIES: *Randy Travis, Ricky Skaggs*
FAVOURITE SPORT: *Squash*
FAVOURITE FILMS: *Ben Hur, Your Cheatin' Heart*
FAVOURITE SONG OR MUSICAL ITEM: *The Blue Danube*
FAVOURITE NON-SHOWBUSINESS PASTIME: *Fishing*
WHO WOULD YOU MOST LIKE TO MEET: *Dolly Parton*
THE QUALITY YOU MOST ADMIRE IN OTHERS: *Personality and honesty*

STAR COMMENT

"You only get out of life what you are prepared to put into it."

PADDY O'BRIEN

Paddy has appeared at many major festivals, including Munich and Vienna

The local pub and cabaret circuit provided Paddy O'Brien with an invaluable musical apprenticeship. With the encouragement of his friends, he recorded a fourteen-track cassette, *Easy Listening* in Fiona Studios, Fermoy, County Cork; it contained many of the Irish favourites he had been performing locally, and sold quite well. At the time he was working as a singer on a part-time basis with a band called The Strangers around the Waterford and South Tipperary region. Even more positive reaction to his subsequent releases, *Memories* and *Favourites*, did enough to convince Paddy he should concentrate his efforts on making a full-time career in show business.

In 1987, still relatively unknown on the national music scene, Paddy was nominated to take part in the Irish final of the European Gold Star Awards, where his performance earned him a highly creditable second place. More than pleased by his success, he vowed to return the following year, and this time he swapped the silver for the gold when he was chosen to represent Ireland in the Gold Star Awards final, held in Holland. Even though he failed to win the major award, Paddy nevertheless performed with distinction and took second place in the "Original Song" category with a composition of his own, *Life Goes Slowly By*. This displayed another side of his talent, and Paddy has since continued the trend by releasing a number of his own compositions, most notably *I'll Always Love You* and *Close To You*.

In 1989 he signed a recording deal with Fáilte Records and released a splendid album called *Making Friends*, distributed in Austria, Switzerland and West Germany, an unusual distinction for an Irish artist. It generated positive media attention for the Country singer from the little village of Aghlish in County Waterford. Although his professional career is still very much in its infancy, Paddy has already gained considerable experience on the international front, having appeared at many major festivals, including Munich and Vienna.

There is no doubt that Paddy O'Brien's musical career is very much on the upturn at this time; good news, indeed, for his steadily increasing following.

PROFILE

HOMEPLACE: *Aghlish, County Waterford*
BIRTHDAY: *November 6*
HEIGHT: *5-10½*
COLOUR OF HAIR: *Fair*
COLOUR OF EYES: *Green*
ABIDING CHILDHOOD MEMORY: *Getting my first radio and having
the independence to listen to Country stations. I remember one Country station in
particular on a foreign channel because they played all the top Country songs.*
EARLY AMBITIONS: *To be involved in some area of music*
FIRST REAL JOB: *Apprentice butcher in Cappoquin Bacon Factory*
EARLIEST RECORDING AND WHEN: *Easy Listening album, 1984*
EARLY MUSICAL INFLUENCES: *Marty Robbins, Brian Coll*
HIGHPOINT IN LIFE TO DATE: *Representing Ireland in the European
Gold Star Awards final in Holland in 1988*
UNFULFILLED AMBITION: *To have a number one hit in the Irish charts*
FAVOURITE IRISH ARTISTS: *Louise Morrissey, John Hogan*
FAVOURITE INTERNATIONAL CELEBRITIES: *Mickey Rourke, Muhammad Ali*
FAVOURITE SPORT: *Gaelic football, hurling*
FAVOURITE FILMS: *Suspect, My Left Foot*
FAVOURITE SONG OR MUSICAL ITEM: *Never Again Will I Knock
On Your Door*
FAVOURITE NON-SHOWBUSINESS PASTIME: *Karate*
WHO WOULD YOU MOST LIKE TO MEET: *Slim Whitman*
THE QUALITY YOU MOST ADMIRE IN OTHERS: *Pleasant personality*

STAR COMMENT

"Live for today, learn from yesterday, and hope for tomorrow."

SALLY O'BRIEN

> *Sally O'Brien brings a homeliness and sincerity to her craft*

Siobhán McGinley can scarcely believe her good fortune. Barely eighteen months ago, Siobhán was performing in the relative anonymity of the pub and cabaret scene around the Derry and Donegal area; today, under the stage name Sally O'Brien, she is making steady progress in the national and international arena.

Siobhán's career transformation began when husband Aidan entered her in a regional heat of the RTE *Live At Three* Search For A Star competition in the Banville House Hotel, Banbridge, County Down. Although she failed to win on the night, Siobhán nevertheless caught the eye of one of the judges, music promoter Tony Loughman, who approached her with a view to recording an album. Almost instantly Siobhán McGinley became Sally O'Brien and, better still, signed a contract leaving all recording matters with Music Box Records and the management side of things to Country Music Management.

Since then awards and accolades, plus recommendations from international Country stars, most notably Porter Wagoner, have become part and parcel of Sally O'Brien's life. In the short space of time since joining the professional ranks, Sally has performed at the Wembley International Country Music Festival and at the Grand Ole Opry, Nashville, on three occasions. In addition Sally's meteoric rise to the higher echelons of the music world is amply demonstrated by her appearances on a number of major television shows in Ireland and America, plus the recording of a duet album and video with Porter Wagoner.

From a family of nine, four boys and five girls, Sally O'Brien, left St Mary's High School in Limavady at sixteen to work in Sherwoods factory in Ballymoney, County Antrim. Subsequently she moved to Derry, and it was while working in Peter England's clothes factory that Siobhán decided to try her luck as a part-time singer with a local band. This led to the formation of a two-piece band, Two Of A Kind, with husband Aidan Canning, and eventually to that much publicised appearance on a talent competition that was to change her life.

Now fronting her own five-piece band, Country Party, Sally O'Brien brings a homeliness and sincerity to her craft so essential to maintaining an affinity with Country and Irish music fans.

PROFILE

HOMEPLACE: *Magilligan, Limavady, County Derry*
BIRTHDAY: *November 7*
HEIGHT: *5-4*
COLOUR OF HAIR: *Sandy*
COLOUR OF EYES: *Blue*
ABIDING CHILDHOOD MEMORY: *Singing at the back of our house in Magilligan and using a mop or brush as a microphone*
EARLY AMBITIONS: *To sing and have a band*
FIRST REAL JOB: *A packer in Sherwood's medical factory in Ballymoney, County Antrim*
EARLIEST RECORDING AND WHEN: *What's Wrong With The Way That We're Doing It Now, 1990 (first recording as Sally O'Brien)*
EARLY MUSICAL INFLUENCES: *Irish showbands, Brian Coll and Philomena Begley*
HIGHPOINT IN LIFE TO DATE: *Recording a duet album, Burning the Midnight Oil, with Porter Wagoner in Nashville*
UNFULFILLED AMBITION: *My ambition to be a singer and have a band has been more than achieved, so I can't say I've an unfulfilled ambition*
FAVOURITE IRISH ARTISTS: *Philomena Begley, Brian Coll*
FAVOURITE INTERNATIONAL CELEBRITIES: *Dolly Parton, Emmylou Harris*
FAVOURITE SPORT: *Squash, badminton*
FAVOURITE FILMS: *Showboat, Calamity Jane*
FAVOURITE SONG OR MUSICAL ITEM: *What's Wrong With The Way We're Doing It Now*
FAVOURITE NON-SHOWBUSINESS PASTIME: *Walking on Benone Beach, Magilligan with my son, Christopher*
WHO WOULD YOU MOST LIKE TO MEET: *Dolly Parton*
THE QUALITY YOU MOST ADMIRE IN OTHERS: *Personality*

STAR COMMENT

"It's great to be alive. Never treat life as a game because it's too short. Live life to the full and accept the bad with the good."

MARY O'CONNOR

Mary now fronts her own London-based band

*T*he first thing you notice about Mary O'Connor when she is performing on stage is how much enjoyment she gets from singing. Her enthusiasm is infectious, and audiences warm to her immediately. No wonder then that Mary has become one of the main attractions on the Country and Irish circuit in England.

Born in London of Irish parents, Mary began her singing career with the Finbar Dwyer Supersound who played around the London area. Even though she was barely a teenager her talent was very much in evidence and Mary soon progressed to lead vocalist with The Magnificent Seven, then resident band at the Forum in Kentish Town.

Some years later Mary decided to make her home in Ireland and continued her career by teaming up with Mick McManus and Country Cousins. Later she joined The Avons under the management of Jimmy Smith, at whose suggestion she changed her stage name to Jenny and tried her hand at Pop. This worked to good effect as she gained national attention with *Who Do You Wanna Be*, a song which later became a Top Ten hit for Gina.

But Mary is first and foremost a Country and Irish singer and it was not long before she came to the attention of Larry Cunningham, who offered her a position with his band. Six years spent with Larry and The Country

Blue Boys propelled Mary to the very top of Irish show business, and even to this day she is closely identified with the famed outfit.

During that period, besides touring America, England and Scotland, Mary recorded three singles, *Letter To Heaven*, *Blue Hills Of Breffni* and *Baby Ride Easy*, a duet with the late Tony Treacy. Mary has since returned to England and now fronts her own London-based band.

Despite her considerable success on the UK scene, Mary is planning to play many more dates here in Ireland in the coming years.

PROFILE

HOMEPLACE: *Hanwell, West London*
BIRTHDAY: *June 20*
HEIGHT: *5-6*
COLOUR OF HAIR: *Dark Brown*
COLOUR OF EYES: *Blue*
ABIDING CHILDHOOD MEMORY: *My first visit to Ireland, the people, the music, the sheer beauty of the country. I fell in love.*
EARLY AMBITIONS: *To be a singer*
FIRST REAL JOB: *Post Office counter clerk*
EARLIEST RECORDING AND WHEN: *Irish Eyes, 1977*
EARLY MUSICAL INFLUENCES: *My father's rendering of Irish ballads, also Margo and Loretta Lynn*
HIGHPOINT IN LIFE TO DATE: *Appearing alongside Val Doonican in concert at the Wembley Conference Centre*
UNFULFILLED AMBITION: *To visit Disneyland and Nashville*
FAVOURITE IRISH ARTISTS: *Mick Flavin, Louise Morrissey*
FAVOURITE INTERNATIONAL CELEBRITIES: *Bob Geldof, Paul McCartney, Bette Midler*
FAVOURITE SPORT: *Gaelic football and soccer*
FAVOURITE FILMS: *What A Wonderful Life, ET*
FAVOURITE SONG OR MUSICAL ITEM: *The Lonesome Boatman*
FAVOURITE NON-SHOWBUSINESS PASTIME: *Bike riding with the kids; badminton*
WHO WOULD YOU MOST LIKE TO MEET: *President Gorbachev*
THE QUALITY YOU MOST ADMIRE IN OTHERS: *I love people who are down to earth and are just themselves*

STAR COMMENT

"Would love to see a massive improvement in Ireland's economy. It's so sad to see all the young people leaving and even sadder to see the situations they can end up in when alone in a strange land. It would be wonderful if, as in the song Flight Of Earls, they could all come back to stay – including me!"

DANIEL O'DONNELL

Daniel has enjoyed unprecedented success on the recording front

*D*aniel O'Donnell is the "Quiet King" of Country and Irish. It is fair to say that, thanks to his enormous talent and personality, he has transformed what some people had regarded as dated and old-fashioned Country and Irish music into the thriving industry it is today. The quiet and unassuming young man from the hills of Donegal has in the space of a few years captured the imagination of the dancing, concert-going and record-buying public and is unquestionably the success story of the Eighties on the Country and Irish music scene.

Daniel's earliest ambition was to be a teacher but a fortuitous meeting with the internationally renowned Up With People organisation while at college in Galway convinced him that he should pursue a career in music. Subsequently Daniel joined his sister Margo as part of her band, and during that useful apprenticeship he got the opportunity to sing a few songs on stage.

Two months prior to leaving Margo's band in 1983 he made his debut as a recording artist by releasing the rather plaintive song, *Donegal Shore*. Although, Daniel was unaware of it, *Donegal Shore* was soon receiving considerable airplay and would become popular in both Ireland and the UK.

The early years as a solo singer were an uphill struggle, but even though he was discouraged at times and thought of leaving the business, Daniel persevered with a single-minded determination which has become one of his hallmarks.

The signing of a contract with Ritz Records should have marked a significant upturn in Daniel's fortunes but he still felt vaguely unhappy about his progress, so much so that he asked for a meeting with Michael Clerkin, managing director of Ritz Productions. These discussions resulted in the formation of a new band, supported by a major publicity promotion under the astute management of Seán Reilly. This was the platform from which Daniel began his climb to the very top of the Irish and British entertainment business. Since then Daniel O'Donnell has become a Country and Irish phenomenon, attracting capacity crowds at virtually every dance and concert venue in Ireland and Britain.

Daniel made his US debut in 1988, where his performance at the Country Music Fan Fare in Nashville was the highlight of the festival. During his stay in Nashville Daniel also appeared as the guest of George Hamilton IV on the famed Grand Ole Opry. Further visits to the home of Country music resulted in appearances on the highly rated *Nashville Now* television show and the recording of a best-selling album, *The Last Waltz*, which was produced by Allen Reynolds at Jack's Tracks Recording Studio.

Then in 1990 Daniel, in his first American concert tour, headlined concerts in Chicago, Boston, Philadelphia and New York's Town Hall. Furthermore, in 1991 Daniel undertook another hugely successful US tour which culminated in a never to be forgotten sell-out show at Carnegie Hall, in New York. Not surprisingly, Daniel is the Irish singer most widely tipped to break big on the American music scene.

Daniel has also enjoyed unprecedented success on the recording front in Ireland and Britain, where every one of his albums have gone straight to number one in the UK Country charts, some of them also earning crossover success in the British Pop charts. While enjoying spectacular record and video sales and capacity audiences at practically every show, Daniel then set his sights on television, and in 1989 hosted a *Country Comes Home* special on RTE. This led eventually to his own ten-programme series, *The Daniel O'Donnell Show*, which featured major Irish and international guests of every musical persuasion. At this moment there seems to be no end to what this man can achieve!

It is no overstatement to suggest that Daniel O'Donnell is likely to go down in history as the man who altered the thinking of a whole generation of Irish music lovers.

PROFILE

HOMEPLACE: Kincasslagh, County Donegal
BIRTHDAY: December 12
HEIGHT: 5-9
COLOUR OF HAIR: Dark Brown
COLOUR OF EYES: Green
ABIDING CHILDHOOD MEMORY: Holidays in Owey Island
EARLY AMBITIONS: To be a teacher
FIRST REAL JOB: Working in the Cope store in Kincasslagh
EARLIEST RECORDING AND WHEN: Donegal Shore/Stand Beside Me, 1983
EARLY MUSICAL INFLUENCES: Mainly Irish music, Jim Reeves,
Hank Williams
HIGHPOINT IN LIFE TO DATE: Meeting Loretta Lynn; becoming Donegal Person
Of The Year, 1989
UNFULFILLED AMBITION: To be on Top Of The Pops
FAVOURITE IRISH ARTISTS: Philomena Begley, Brian Coll
FAVOURITE INTERNATIONAL CELEBRITIES: Loretta Lynn, Charley Pride
FAVOURITE SPORT: Tenpin bowling
FAVOURITE FILMS: The Quiet Man, The Sound Of Music, Madame X
FAVOURITE SONG OR MUSICAL ITEM: The Rose
FAVOURITE NON-SHOWBUSINESS PASTIME: Tenpin bowling
WHO WOULD YOU MOST LIKE TO MEET: Pope John Paul II
THE QUALITY YOU MOST ADMIRE IN OTHERS: Friendliness

STAR COMMENT

"A stranger is a friend you do not know."

KEVIN PRENDERGAST

Kevin has built up a reputation as a first-rate songwriter

To those familiar with his music, it should come as no surprise to learn that singer-songwriter Kevin Prendergast is a reluctant emigrant. Many of his songs tell of the heartbreak of emigration, which Kevin himself has endured over the years.

Reared on a small farm in County Mayo, Kevin began his schooldays in Logboy and later attended the Technical School in nearby Ballyhaunis. Like so many who grew up in rural Ireland in the Sixties, Kevin spent much of his summer holidays making the hay and saving the turf. His was an idyllic childhood. There were no thoughts then of ever having to leave home but eventually the situation had to be faced and Kevin found himself working as a barman in Manchester.

He found comfort in music and soon Kevin began performing in pubs and clubs around the North of England. Thereafter, he returned every summer to the West of Ireland where he built up a sizeable following on the cabaret scene. It was during one of those working holidays that Kevin successfully auditioned for the position of singer on *Céilí House*, the popular RTE Radio programme. This newfound status proved very beneficial to his career as it afforded him the opportunity to perform live on national radio about six times a year.

Kevin's first release, the self-penned, *Let's Go Back To Mayo*, demonstrated his considerable talents as a Country and Irish singer. Since that early recording, Kevin has released five albums and numerous singles, all in his own distinctive style.

Through the years Kevin has built up a reputation as a first-rate song-writer and has written many popular favourites including: *The Lady We Call Mother, I'll Sing About Roscommon, Three Trophies For Our Country, Peace To All The Nations* and *Susan, Phil and Margo*. No doubt there are many more fine songs to come from this singing Irish emigrant.

PROFILE

HOMEPLACE: Carramack, Tulrahan, Ballyhaunis, County Mayo
BIRTHDAY: July 29
HEIGHT: 5-7
COLOUR OF HAIR: Brown
COLOUR OF EYES: Blue
ABIDING CHILDHOOD MEMORY: Growing up on a little farm in Mayo
EARLY AMBITIONS: To become a priest
FIRST REAL JOB: Apprentice barman
EARLIEST RECORDING AND WHEN: Let's Go Back To Mayo, 1981
EARLY MUSICAL INFLUENCES: Bridie Gallagher, Brian Coll
HIGHPOINT IN LIFE TO DATE: Writing and recording my first song
UNFULFILLED AMBITION: To sing in Australia
FAVOURITE IRISH ARTISTS: Big Tom, Bridie Gallagher
FAVOURITE INTERNATIONAL CELEBRITIES: Charley Pride, George Best
FAVOURITE SPORT: Gaelic football, soccer
FAVOURITE FILMS: The Quiet Man, The Sound Of Music
FAVOURITE SONG OR MUSICAL ITEM: The Boys From The County Mayo
FAVOURITE NON-SHOWBUSINESS PASTIME: Sightseeing around Ireland
WHO WOULD YOU MOST LIKE TO MEET: Pope John Paul II
THE QUALITY YOU MOST ADMIRE IN OTHERS: Honesty and respectfulness

STAR COMMENT

"Work hard and always be ready to help others."

BRENDAN QUINN

One of the finest Country singers in Ireland today

*I*nspired by his older sister, Philomena, Brendan Quinn was determined to become involved in some area of show business from a very early age. At the time, Philomena sang with The Malachy Doris Céilí Band, and Brendan often listened to them in admiration. The ambitious youngster didn't have long to wait. Seán McKee, then lead vocalist of a local County Derry skiffle group, promised Brendan a job on condition that he learned to play the guitar, just the incentive to get any youngster working hard. He purchased a guitar and, after Seán had taught him the initial chords, spent many months mastering the intricacies of the instrument. Consequently, he was a proficient guitarist when, as he was promised, he teamed up with the local band.

During the following years, Brendan pursued two separate careers, one as an apprentice fitter/welder, the other as a part-time musician with Seán's newly named group, The Breakaways, which played support to many of the big-name showband stars, including Joe Dolan, Brendan Bowyer and Brian Coll. When in 1967 Robin Averill emigrated to Canada, Brendan was chosen as lead vocalist of The Breakaways, and took the opportunity to record his first single, *Help Me Make It Through The Night*. In 1972 Brendan reached number five in the Irish charts with a splendid version of *Four In The Morning*, which many people still identify with his voice.

After leaving The Breakaways to form his own band, The Blue Birds, Brendan still continued to release hit singles like *Behind Closed Doors*, *To Daddy*, *Wedding Bells*, *I Can Almost See My Home Town From Here*, and *Daddy's Little Girl*, a number one in 1975. They appeared for four successive years at the Wembley International County Music Festival and also toured America with such Country greats as Don Williams and Merle Haggard.

In 1981 a lucrative offer to tour Canada for fourteen weeks brought about big changes in Brendan's life. He was so taken with the international music scene that he spent four years abroad. Since his return to Ireland he has been playing many of the major venues and co-hosted the popular *Make Mine Country* series on BBC television for two seasons; suitable recognition for one of the finest Country singers in Ireland today.

PROFILE

HOMEPLACE: *Magherafelt, County Derry*
BIRTHDAY: *December 19*
HEIGHT: *5-7*
COLOUR OF HAIR: *Brown/Grey*
COLOUR OF EYES: *Blue*
ABIDING CHILDHOOD MEMORY: *Being left off the bus with my sister, Bridget, at Gulladuff and having to walk the three miles to my granny's farm in Drummuck with a heavy suitcase, so we stuck a big stick through the handle and carried it that way*
EARLY AMBITIONS: *To play music*
FIRST REAL JOB: *Apprentice fitter/welder*
EARLIEST RECORDING AND WHEN: *Help Me Make It Through The Night, 1969*
EARLY MUSICAL INFLUENCES: *The Beatles, Buck Owens, Merle Haggard*
HIGHPOINT IN LIFE TO DATE: *Winning the Tulsa, Oklahoma, Mayfest in 1980*
UNFULFILLED AMBITION: *To give my family a good education and prepare them properly for the future*
FAVOURITE IRISH ARTISTS: *Brian Coll, Mary Black*
FAVOURITE INTERNATIONAL CELEBRITIES: *Muhammad Ali, Tony Benn MP*
FAVOURITE SPORT: *Gaelic football, soccer*
FAVOURITE FILMS: *High Noon, The Deerhunter*
FAVOURITE SONG OR MUSICAL ITEM: *Cool Water*
FAVOURITE NON-SHOWBUSINESS PASTIME: *Watching current affairs programmes*
WHO WOULD YOU MOST LIKE TO MEET: *Van Morrison*
THE QUALITY YOU MOST ADMIRE IN OTHERS: *Honesty*

STAR COMMENT

"Be honest and take everybody as you meet them, as no two people are alike."

PADDY REILLY

He continues to tour the world, singing powerful songs in his own inimitable style

*B*allad singing of the highest standard has long been Paddy Reilly's trademark. Yet for over twenty years major success eluded him. Then in 1983 it all came right when Paddy recorded the Pete St John composition, *The Fields Of Athenry*, a recording which not only became a massive chart hit but also proved to be one of the best-selling Irish records ever.

Although Paddy had experienced chart success nine years earlier with *The Town I Loved So Well*, which had three stays in the Irish charts over a five-year period, it was undoubtedly *The Fields Of Athenry* that elevated him from pub and club performer to theatre and concert star. This new-found status was never more in evidence than at a concert in Melbourne in 1987 when Paddy played to a capacity crowd of over five thousand. In addition, *Paddy Reilly's Ireland* album, featuring one song from every county in Ireland, as well as being a best seller here at home sold in excess of 50,000 copies in Canada, where Paddy is now a major concert star.

Paddy's first love was jazz and, as a youngster growing up in Rathcoole, he liked nothing better than listening to his favourite music on the US radio network, The Voice Of America. His early years were spent working as an assistant machinist in the paper mills in Saggart, and at that time a career in music seemed far away. However, Mick McCarthy, who then owned The Embankment – a popular music haunt in Dublin – asked Paddy to sing a few songs in his lounge. Prior to that Paddy used to sing in the adjacent bar just for the fun of it. The inclusion of some of those songs on a compilation album that also featured such artists as Danny Doyle, Al O'Donnell, Olive Boyle and James Keane, brought him to a wider audience and, thereafter, he became a regular fixture on the club and pub scene around Dublin.

In May 1987 Paddy recorded *The Flight Of Earls* which became a major summer hit, topping the Irish charts in the process. Besides recording, he continues to tour the world, singing powerful songs in his own inimitable style. It may have taken a long time but, after twenty-five years on the road, Paddy Reilly has at last become a major success.

PROFILE

HOMEPLACE: *Rathcoole, County Dublin*
BIRTHDAY: *October 18*
HEIGHT: *5-10*
COLOUR OF HAIR: *Greying*
COLOUR OF EYES: *Blue*
ABIDING CHILDHOOD MEMORY: *The great excitement in Rathcoole when Mr What won the Grand National; the horse was trained in Rathcoole by Tom Taaffe and there was tremendous excitement in the village for weeks afterwards*
EARLY AMBITIONS: *To be a doctor*
FIRST REAL JOB: *Apprentice mechanic*
EARLIEST RECORDING AND WHEN: *The Curragh Of Kildare, 1962*
EARLY MUSICAL INFLUENCES: *Jussi Bjorling and Maria Callas*
HIGHPOINT IN LIFE TO DATE: *Performing in Carnegie Hall, New York*
UNFULFILLED AMBITION: *To go off on a space shuttle*
FAVOURITE IRISH ARTISTS: *Stocktons Wing, Virginia Kerr*
FAVOURITE INTERNATIONAL CELEBRITIES: *Maradona, Paul Scofield*
FAVOURITE SPORT: *Gaelic football, hurling*
FAVOURITE FILMS: *The Producers, A Man For All Seasons*
FAVOURITE SONG OR MUSICAL ITEM: *La Boheme*
FAVOURITE NON-SHOWBUSINESS PASTIME: *Attending race meetings*
WHO WOULD YOU MOST LIKE TO MEET: *Sophia Loren*
THE QUALITY YOU MOST ADMIRE IN OTHERS: *Honesty*

STAR COMMENT

"Life is very precious so enjoy it while you have it."

DICKIE ROCK

> *Dickie Rock is above all else a vocal stylist*

*D*ickie Rock, one of the most influential singers ever in Irish music, is above all else a vocal stylist. Indeed, ever since his powerful version of *There's Always Me* rocketed to number one in the Irish charts in 1963, Dickie has remained a firm favourite with record buyers and dancers alike. A consummate professional, his major hits have included *I'm Yours, From The Candy Store On The Corner, Come Back To Stay, Simon Says, Wishing It Was You, Every Step Of The Way, There's Always Me* and *Back Home*.

Dickie Rock's musical development began in earnest when at a very early age he joined the local church choir in Cabra West in Dublin. Subsequently he became a member of The Casino Players, an amateur variety group who entertained at various hospitals around the city. However, it was while serving his time as an apprentice welder that Dickie got his first real break in the music business when he was asked to join The Mellow Chords, who were searching for a lead vocalist at the time. One of his workmates – who played with the band – had heard Dickie singing and was suitably impressed. Interestingly, the singer who Dickie replaced was none other than Butch Moore, who later became lead vocalist with The Capitol Showband.

Some years later Dickie approached Tom Doherty, then manager of The Miami, to seek professional management for his newly formed band,

The Echoes. As it happened, The Miami were without a lead singer and, instead of finding a manager for his fledgling band, Dickie, after a successful audition in the Palm Beach, Portmarnock, became lead singer of The Miami. It was the beginning of a musical legend.

In 1966 Dickie represented Ireland in the Eurovision Song Contest, finishing fourth with *Come Back To Stay*, a song which became a massive hit in the Irish charts.

In the intevening years Dickie Rock, having formed his own band in 1972, has enjoyed enormous popularity and must surely rate as one of most professional and dedicated entertainers ever to grace the Irish music scene.

PROFILE

HOMEPLACE: Cabra West, Dublin
BIRTHDAY: September 10
HEIGHT: 5-10
COLOUR OF HAIR: Brown
COLOUR OF EYES: Brown
ABIDING CHILDHOOD MEMORY: The closeness of our family;
seaside outings
EARLY AMBITIONS: None in particular
FIRST REAL JOB: Working in a jeweller's shop in Talbot Street, Dublin
EARLIEST RECORDING AND WHEN: There's Always Me, 1963
EARLY MUSICAL INFLUENCES: Frank Sinatra, Jerry Lee Lewis
HIGHPOINT IN LIFE TO DATE: Representing Ireland in the Eurovision Song
Contest, 1966
UNFULFILLED AMBITION: To have an international hit record
FAVOURITE IRISH ARTISTS: Joe Dolan, Red Hurley, Mary Black
FAVOURITE INTERNATIONAL CELEBRITIES: Frank Sinatra,
Barbara Streisand
FAVOURITE SPORT: Soccer and snooker
FAVOURITE FILMS: The Godfather 1 and 2
FAVOURITE SONG OR MUSICAL ITEM: My Way, Nessun Dorma
FAVOURITE NON-SHOWBUSINESS PASTIME: Snooker
WHO WOULD YOU MOST LIKE TO MEET: Frank Sinatra
THE QUALITY YOU MOST ADMIRE IN OTHERS: Honesty and loyalty

STAR COMMENT

"Life is not a rehearsal."

BRENDAN SHINE

Brendan shows no signs of easing up

*T*he mantle of entertainer extraordi-naire rests easily on the broad shoulders of Brendan Shine. Not for him the high life of a superstar. Brendan, the man who has had most hits in the Irish charts – with the exception of Cliff Richard and Elvis Presley – derives as much enjoyment from being at home on the family farm near Athlone as he gets from striding the stage, accordion in hand, at major venues both in Ireland and abroad.

Brendan is much more than the father-figure of Irish show business. He is also a man of vision, having strong views on subjects as diverse as his beloved music, farming, sport and emigration. He is particularly saddened that we seem to have lost much of our nation's culture, but he feels strongly that, eventually, people will go back to their roots and that the community centre will become the accepted meeting place for the local populace.

Although born in Portarlington, County Laois, where his father was a transport foreman, Brendan's family returned to the homeplace in Kielty in South Roscommon when Brendan was still very young. He enjoyed a rich musical upbringing and began playing the organ in the local Drum church when barely eleven. Soon his prowess as a musician and singer made him a very popular performer at functions around the locality before he joined his father's band. Some time later Brendan teamed up with the famous Kieran Kelly Céilí Band as lead vocalist. The experience proved invaluable when, some years later, he left to front his own band.

In 1971 Brendan reached number one in the Irish charts with the novelty number, *O'Brien Has No Place To Go.* He continued to top the charts with great regularity during the following years. His best-known song, the one with which most people associate him, spent a staggering thirty-seven weeks in the Irish charts: *Do You Want Your Old Lobby Washed Down.* And just about everybody knows it.

Brendan, fast approaching thirty years in the music business, shows no signs of easing up. Hopefully, he'll be singing those old familiar standards for many years to come.

PROFILE

HOMEPLACE: Woodville, Kielty, County Roscommon
BIRTHDAY: June 2
HEIGHT: 6.00½
COLOUR OF HAIR: Fair
COLOUR OF EYES: Blue
ABIDING CHILDHOOD MEMORY: I was running around a corner and ran into another fellow and as a result I had a black eye for my Confirmation
EARLY AMBITIONS: To be a chef
FIRST REAL JOB: Singer with The Kieran Kelly Céilí Band
EARLIEST RECORDING AND WHEN: Treat Me Daughter Kindly, 1967
EARLY MUSICAL INFLUENCES: Connie Foley, George Jones
HIGHPOINT IN LIFE TO DATE: Interviewing Cardinal Tomás O Fiach (RIP) on Saturday Live. I was very impressed with him as a man. I was so thrilled that he would answer my invitation to appear on my programme and that he would chat so normally to me.
UNFULFILLED AMBITION: To have a Top Forty hit in the British charts
FAVOURITE IRISH ARTISTS: Mary Black, Joe Dolan
FAVOURITE INTERNATIONAL CELEBRITIES: Bono, President Gorbachev
FAVOURITE SPORT: Gaelic football
FAVOURITE FILMS: Straw Dogs, Crocodile Dundee
FAVOURITE SONG OR MUSICAL ITEM: Do You Want Your Old Lobby Washed Down
FAVOURITE NON-SHOWBUSINESS PASTIME: Farming
WHO WOULD YOU MOST LIKE TO MEET: Pope John Paul II
THE QUALITY YOU MOST ADMIRE IN OTHERS: Sincerity, stamina and honesty

STAR COMMENT

"In music never outstep your capabilities and always be honest and please the people that pay to see you. In other words, give value for money."

TONY STEVENS

> *It seems only a matter of time before Tony Stevens gains international attention*

*T*ony Stevens has few peers as a vocalist on the Irish music scene, a fact acknowledged by record buyers and patrons alike.

The Cork-born singer has been involved with music since schooldays when he attended the CBS in Sullivan's Quay in his home city. But it was from listening to Radio Luxembourg during the 1960s that, like so many of his contemporaries, Tony first developed an interest in the music of that era.

Indeed, it was shortly after hearing The Beatles' hit song, *Daytripper*, on Radio Luxembourg that the young Tony listened in awe as local Cork band, The Martells, featured the song in their repertoire. After that he could settle for nothing but a musical career. He formed a five-piece band with his school friends and learned the trade by playing support to many of the big-name stars of the day. This brought him to the position of lead vocalist with Western Union. Some years later Tony released what many still regard as one of his best-ever singles, *Send Me No Roses*, which claimed substantial airplay on RTE Radio 1.

Since then Tony has achieved an enormous amount of success both on the Irish and international scene. He scooped first prize in a major bi-centennial song contest in Sydney, and two years later won the top award at the Bratislava Song Contest in Czechoslovakia. When his great version of *The Village Of Asdee* made the Irish charts in 1983, Tony was presented with a special award by the residents of the small Kerry town which he had immortalised in song.

Today, Tony Stevens continues to delight highly appreciative audiences with his ultra-professional stage performances. His repertoire consists of all his past hits, plus some excellent cover versions of many of the Country, Rock and Roll and golden oldies favourites.

Considering his abundant talent and flair, it seems only a matter of time before Tony Stevens gains international attention. When that happens it will be a well-deserved honour for the genial singer from "The Banks".

PROFILE

HOMEPLACE: *Ballinlough, Cork City*
BIRTHDAY: *July 22*
HEIGHT: *5-10*
COLOUR OF HAIR: *Fair*
COLOUR OF EYES: *Blue*
ABIDING CHILDHOOD MEMORY: *Winning a hurling medal with Blackrock Hurling Club in Cork at the age of eight. A club member asked me to play as they were short a player. Even though I'd never hit a ball, he brought me on the crossbar of the bike to the club where I got togged out in all the gear. After all that, the other team never turned up so I won a medal without ever playing at all!*
EARLY AMBITIONS: *To join a band*
FIRST REAL JOB: *Salesman in a shoe shop*
EARLIEST RECORDING AND WHEN: *Send Me No Roses, 1976*
EARLY MUSICAL INFLUENCES: *Elvis Presley, The Beatles*
HIGHPOINT IN LIFE TO DATE: *Representing Ireland in the Bratislava Song Contest in Czechoslovakia*
UNFULFILLED AMBITION: *To have an international number one*
FAVOURITE IRISH ARTISTS: *Red Hurley, Philomena Begley*
FAVOURITE INTERNATIONAL CELEBRITIES: *Robert Redford, Willie Nelson*
FAVOURITE SPORT: *Swimming*
FAVOURITE FILMS: *The Great Escape, A Fish Called Wanda*
FAVOURITE SONG OR MUSICAL ITEM: *How About Us*
FAVOURITE NON-SHOWBUSINESS PASTIME: *Fishing*
WHO WOULD YOU MOST LIKE TO MEET: *Dudley Moore*
THE QUALITY YOU MOST ADMIRE IN OTHERS: *Honesty*

STAR COMMENT

"A new brush sweeps clean but the old one knows the corners."

GENE STUART

Gene Stuart has a distinctive country style all his own

*F*or over twenty years Gene Stuart has been happily performing as a professional entertainer of skill and flair. It seems as though there never was a time when Gene wasn't earning his living as a stage performer, but nothing could be further from the truth. His entry into the top flight of show business came more by accident than design. Having left school when he was just thirteen and served his time as a barman, he worked as a sales representative before taking the emigrant ship to Britain in the mid-Sixties. Like many before him, young Eugene worked on building sites as a labourer, earning the princely sum of £21 for a seven-day week.

During a short visit home he secured work as a freelance photographer at *The Dungannon Observer* newspaper. Some time later he was auditioned for lead vocalist with The Mighty Avons who were searching for a quality singer to replace Larry Cunningham, and he was offered the position.

Then in January 1970 his first song, *Before The Next Teardrop Falls*, enjoyed a lengthy stay in the Irish charts, peaking at number three. In the years that followed, Gene notched up one chart success after another with *I'd Rather Love and Lose You*, *Don't Go*, *I'm Just Lucky I Guess*, and *Kiss An Angel Good Morning*, all special highpoints in his career.

An unexpected two-month stay in hospital, followed by a six-month convalescence, brought many changes in Gene's life. He left The Mighty

Avons and formed his own band, The Homesteaders, and together they have been performing on the ballroom and cabaret circuit with considerable success.

Gene Stuart has a distinctive country style all his own which makes it easy to understand why he has remained such a firm favourite through the years.

PROFILE

HOMEPLACE: *Lisnagleer, Dungannon, County Tyrone*
BIRTHDAY: *May 16*
HEIGHT: *6-1*
COLOUR OF HAIR: *Brown*
COLOUR OF EYES: *Blue*
ABIDING CHILDHOOD MEMORY: *My first day going to school on the carrier of my mother's bike*
EARLY AMBITIONS: *To be a priest*
FIRST REAL JOB: *Apprentice barman*
EARLIEST RECORDING AND WHEN: *Sing The Blues To Daddy, 1969*
EARLY MUSICAL INFLUENCES: *Jim Reeves*
HIGHPOINT IN LIFE TO DATE: *Being chosen to replace Larry Cunningham as lead vocalist with The Mighty Avons*
UNFULFILLED AMBITION: *To play a part on television in RTE's most popular 'soap', Glenroe*
FAVOURITE IRISH ARTISTS: *Frank McCaffrey, Sheila Barry*
FAVOURITE INTERNATIONAL CELEBRITIES: *Cliff Thorburn, Dean Martin*
FAVOURITE SPORT: *Gaelic football*
FAVOURITE FILMS: *Sons Of Katie Elder, Rio Bravo*
FAVOURITE SONG OR MUSICAL ITEM: *Ol' Black Joe*
FAVOURITE NON-SHOWBUSINESS PASTIME: *Snooker, pool*
WHO WOULD YOU MOST LIKE TO MEET: *Pope John Paul II*
THE QUALITY YOU MOST ADMIRE IN OTHERS: *Humility*

STAR COMMENT

"Be nice to each other."

T I N A

> **Nowadays Tina is one of our foremost cabaret artists**

Sweet-singing Tina is one of the few overnight success stories in the history of Irish show business. It started when she won a talent competition in Butlins Holiday Camp in Skegness, in England. Her local newspaper, *The Wicklow People*, featured the story and it caught the eye of Tom Cranny, then manager of The Mexicans. A telegram from Tom – now sadly deceased – brought her back to Ireland and telephonist Philomena Quinn was launched on the Irish music scene as Tina, a new showband attraction. Subsequently she built up a reputation as a quality singer able to perform any kind of song, no matter how difficult.

There followed four very successful years, during which time Tina and The Mexicans toured extensively, taking in the UK and Germany. In 1968 she teamed up with Big Jim Farley and The Top Hatters, and in time became lead vocalist with The Real McCoy, with whom she enjoyed her first number one hit, *I Don't Know How To Love Him*, in 1971. That, too, was the year in which she was voted 'Number One Female Singer' by the readers of *New Spotlight Magazine*, a distinction she won a second time in 1974. That same year Tina represented Ireland in the Eurovision Song Contest, with the Paul Lyttle composition, *Cross Your Heart*, having already emerged victorious in the Gibraltar Song Contest with her superb interpretation of *Sugar Daddy*.

However, the highpoint of her career was the Eurovision Song Contest in which she finished a creditable joint fifth behind the eventual winners, Abba. Shortly after Eurovision Tina was on the move again, this time to The Nevada. She continued to record some splendid material and entered the Irish charts with the appropriately titled, *I'll Do It All Again*. Despite suffering severe injuries as a result of two car accidents, the second of which kept her out of work for over eighteen months, Tina likes nothing better than traversing the country roads, bringing her own special blend of magic to her many fans.

Nowadays Tina is one of our foremost cabaret artists and is singing as well as at any other time in her eventful career.

PROFILE

HOMEPLACE: *Greystones, County Wicklow*
BIRTHDAY: *April 21*
HEIGHT: *5-0*
COLOUR OF HAIR: *Blonde*
COLOUR OF EYES: *Hazel*
ABIDING CHILDHOOD MEMORY: *My sister and myself being taken by our father out into the fields to help him with his work. But instead we'd skip off and spend the time picking primroses and bluebells.*
EARLY AMBITIONS: *To be a nun*
FIRST REAL JOB: *Telephonist*
EARLIEST RECORDING AND WHEN: *I Won't Marry Him Today, 1965*
EARLY MUSICAL INFLUENCES: *The Everly Brothers*
HIGHPOINT IN LIFE TO DATE: *Representing Ireland in the Eurovision Song Contest in 1974*
UNFULFILLED AMBITION: *To visit Medjugorje and Rome*
FAVOURITE IRISH ARTISTS: *Ray Lynam, Gina*
FAVOURITE INTERNATIONAL CELEBRITIES: *Nat King Cole, Frank Sinatra*
FAVOURITE SPORT: *Swimming*
FAVOURITE FILMS: *Gone With The Wind, The Nun's Story*
FAVOURITE SONG OR MUSICAL ITEM: *Whiter Shade Of Pale*
FAVOURITE NON-SHOWBUSINESS PASTIME: *Walking*
WHO WOULD YOU MOST LIKE TO MEET: *Mother Teresa*
THE QUALITY YOU MOST ADMIRE IN OTHERS: *Truthfulness*

STAR COMMENT

"Be your natural self."

TWO'S COMPANY FIVE

I know what it is to have money and what it's like to be broke

Well over twenty years ago Eamonn McRory from Dungannon, County Tyrone and County Carlow-born Mary Darcy came together to form Two's Company. Neither Eamonn, an ex-motor mechanic, nor Mary, who had been living in Birmingham with her family for a number of years, could have foreseen how successful the partnership would become.

They had met in a pub where Eamonn was appearing one night and Mary, a member of the audience, had been requested to sing. This marked the beginning of a remarkable duet and they played their first engagement in The Embankment, Tallaght. Eamonn had played with various bands, including Frankie McBride and The Polka Dots, before teaming up with Mary who, during her Birmingham days, had sung with a resident group in that city.

In 1969 Two's Company enjoyed a lengthy stay in the Irish charts with *Eileen McManus*, and more chart successes followed with *Dear John, You're My Best Friend* and *Live Like Hell*. Then came several albums, one of which was produced by Porter Wagoner in Nashville, where they also appeared at the Grand Ole Opry in 1981. They subsequently recorded two television series of *Nice N' Easy* with Brendan Shine and, besides winning several Country Music awards as Ireland's most popular duo, Eamonn and Mary were also selected as Best International Duo which earned them an appearance at a major festival in Fort Worth, Texas.

Furthermore, they had the distinction of being the first duo to represent Ireland at the European Gold Star Awards in Holland in 1983. They also toured America twice yearly for six successive years during the Seventies. Greatly influenced by her parents, Bill and Sinead, Mary learned to appreciate music at an early age and, with the help of music teacher Cyril Jolly, soon became a proficient accordionist. When in 1964 her family moved to Birmingham to be with their father, who was working there at the time, Mary continued her musical interests by teaming up with her father in the Slieve Bloom Céilí Band. Mary remained with the Céilí Band for about six months, then spent over a year as lead singer with a resident group in the Four Provinces, Kings Heath, before returning to Ireland and that chance meeting with Eamonn.

Eamonn McRory started off singing as a boy soprano in the local church choir under the guidance of Brother Oliver of the Presentation Brothers, Dungannon. Around that time, too, the young Eamonn played with the family vocal group before becoming a member of a ballroom orchestra at the age of sixteen. However, music took a back seat when, about a year later, Eamonn moved to England and joined the Air Force, where he trained as a mechanic. For some time after returning home Eamonn sampled different types of work, including that of rhythm guitarist with The Grafton Showband and The Polka Dots. Eventually, though, he secured work as a mechanic in Carlow and began playing solo on a part-time basis around the local pub circuit.

In the summer of 1991, in order to widen their appeal to cabaret and dancing audiences, Eamonn and Mary formed a five-piece band, Two's Company Five, the three additions comprising Paul Quinlan, Jimmy Byrne and Mary's youngest brother, Seán Darcy, who was just six months old when Two's Company played their first date.

PROFILE

EAMONN McRORY
HOMEPLACE: Dungannon, County Tyrone
BIRTHDAY: January 10
HEIGHT: 6.00½
COLOUR OF HAIR: Silver grey
COLOUR OF EYES: Blue
ABIDING CHILDHOOD MEMORY: Visiting Belfast after the blitz
EARLY AMBITIONS: To be a Rock and Roll singer
FIRST REAL JOB: Box-making machinist
EARLIEST RECORDING AND WHEN: Eileen McManus, 1969
EARLY MUSICAL INFLUENCES: Dolly Parton, Porter Wagoner, Buck Owens
HIGHPOINT IN LIFE TO DATE: Appearing on The Grand Ole Opry
UNFULFILLED AMBITION: To host my own TV series
FAVOURITE IRISH ARTISTS: Philomena Begley, Mick Flavin
FAVOURITE INTERNATIONAL CELEBRITIES: Freddy Starr, Russ Abbott,

Kenny Rogers
FAVOURITE SPORT: Soccer
FAVOURITE FILMS: Where Eagles Dare, Rhinestone
FAVOURITE SONG OR MUSICAL ITEM: The Town I Loved So Well
FAVOURITE NON-SHOWBUSINESS PASTIME: DIY, gardening
WHO WOULD YOU MOST LIKE TO MEET: Jack Charlton
THE QUALITY YOU MOST ADMIRE IN OTHERS: Stamina

STAR COMMENT

"I've had thirty years in the business as a semi-professional and professional entertainer. I've had good times and bad; had highs and lows. I know what it is to have money and what it's like to be broke. I know what it's like to be happy and what it's like to be sad. I've been sick and I've been well; had success and failure. I've experienced life from all angles and the only thing I'm sure of is that if I could re-live those thirty years I wouldn't change one second of them. I enjoy being alive."

PROFILE

MARY DARCY

HOMEPLACE: Rathvilly, County Carlow
BIRTHDAY: December 9
HEIGHT: 5-7
COLOUR OF HAIR: Auburn
COLOUR OF EYES: Brown
ABIDING CHILDHOOD MEMORY: Getting a glimpse of Maisie McDaniel who, at the time, was one of Ireland's most popular entertainers. I remember she came to sing at the carnival in Rathvilly and was invited to the parochial house by my aunt who was the housekeeper. It was a great thrill to catch sight of her as she was my idol. I made up my mind there and then to try to be a singer like Maisie.
EARLY AMBITIONS: To be a singer in a band
FIRST REAL JOB: Working as a hairdresser in Birmingham
EARLIEST RECORDING AND WHEN: Eileen McManus, 1969
EARLY MUSICAL INFLUENCES: Dolly Parton, Porter Wagoner, Maisie McDaniel
HIGHPOINT IN LIFE TO DATE: Appearing at the Grand Ole Opry
UNFULFILLED AMBITION: To have my own TV series
FAVOURITE IRISH ARTISTS: Frank McCaffrey, Louise Morrissey
FAVOURITE INTERNATIONAL CELEBRITIES: Kenny Rogers, Tanya Tucker
FAVOURITE SPORT: Tennis
FAVOURITE FILMS: The Sound Of Music, An Officer And A Gentleman
FAVOURITE SONG OR MUSICAL ITEM: I Have A Dream (Abba)
FAVOURITE NON-SHOWBUSINESS PASTIME: Shopping
WHO WOULD YOU MOST LIKE TO MEET: Pope John Paul II
THE QUALITY YOU MOST ADMIRE IN OTHERS: Kindness

STAR COMMENT

"Two's Company have been on the road now for twenty-three years and we've had some very good times. Sometimes through frustration or otherwise, I've threatened to pack it all in, but we've made some very good friendships that have lasted and still go on today. I've enjoyed my life on the road and really couldn't see myself doing anything else. Thanks to all our fans and I hope they continue to come and see us over the next twenty-three years."

THE WOLFE TONES

> **Such is their popularity, they have been given the freedom of both New York and Los Angeles**

*T*he Wolfe Tones have done it all. Since their formation in 1963 they have enjoyed success after success in top-of-the-bill concert tours that have taken them all over the globe to such venues as Carnegie Hall in New York, the Olympia Theatre in Paris and the Albert Hall in London.

The group had its beginning in Inchicore, Dublin, when brothers Derek and Brian Warfield and neighbour, Noel Nagle, decided it was time to bring their blend of music to nationwide audiences. Subsequently the trio featured at clubs and fleadhs all over the country and it was at a fleadh in Elphin, County Roscommon, that they met and befriended another Dubliner, Tommy Byrne. It was a meeting that was to change their lives. The lads were so impressed with Tommy's skill as a vocalist and musician that they immediately invited him to join the group. A short time later all four abandoned their day jobs and became professional musicians. Since then, the talented foursome have recorded over fifteen hugely successful albums and numerous memorable singles like *Streets Of New York*, which reached the top of the Irish charts in 1981, and songs like *Slievenamon, James Connolly, Snowy Breasted Pearl, On The One Road, Farewell To Dublin* and *Irish Eyes*.

Twenty-eight years on, The Wolfe Tones still continue to tour regularly, spending two months of each year in America where, such is their popularity, they have been given the freedom of both New York and Los Angeles.

Despite spectacular international success, The Wolfe Tones like nothing better than returning to Ireland every summer and meeting their fans at all the major cabaret and concert venues.

It is a source of great pride to The Wolfe Tones that they are a major act in their own country. More than any other achievement, that is what matters most of all.

PROFILE

TOMMY BYRNE

HOMEPLACE: *Thomas's Road, Donore Avenue, Dublin*
BIRTHDAY: *March 23*
HEIGHT: *6.00*
COLOUR OF HAIR: *Brown*
COLOUR OF EYES: *Blue*
ABIDING CHILDHOOD MEMORY: *Playing street games*
EARLY AMBITIONS: *To travel; I always hiked and cycled and wanted to see the world*
FIRST REAL JOB: *Messenger boy in Guinness Brewery*
EARLIEST RECORDING AND WHEN: *Single: Down In The Mines; album: Foggy Dew, 1965*
EARLY MUSICAL INFLUENCES: *Joan Baez*
HIGHPOINT IN LIFE TO DATE: *All Irish successes in show business and sport*
UNFULFILLED AMBITION: *To slow down and enjoy life with my family*
FAVOURITE IRISH ARTISTS: *Joe Dolan, Mary Coughlan*
FAVOURITE INTERNATIONAL CELEBRITIES: *Seve Ballesteros, Frank Stapleton*
FAVOURITE SPORT: *Golf, soccer, hurling*
FAVOURITE FILMS: *The Great Escape, One Flew Over The Cuckoo's Nest*
FAVOURITE SONG OR MUSICAL ITEM: *First Of May (José Feliciano)*
FAVOURITE NON-SHOWBUSINESS PASTIME: *Golf, sea angling*
WHO WOULD YOU MOST LIKE TO MEET: *Sophia Loren*
THE QUALITY YOU MOST ADMIRE IN OTHERS: *Sincerity*

STAR COMMENT

"I'm delighted to have been successful in my own country."